Stop-motion Animation

Frame by Frame Film-making with Puppets and Models

Second edition

Fairchild Books
An imprint of Bloomsbury Publishing Plc

50 Bedford Square
London
WC1B 3DP
UK

1385 Broadway
New York
NY 10018
USA

www.bloomsbury.com

Bloomsbury is a registered trade mark of Bloomsbury
Publishing Plc
First published 2014
© Bloomsbury Publishing Plc, 2014

British Library Cataloguing-in-Publication Data

A catalogue record for this book is available from the
British Library
ISBN: PB: 978-1-4725-2190-3
ePDF: 978-1-4725-3943-4

Library of Congress Cataloging-in-Publication Data
Purves, Barry.
Stop-motion Animation: Frame by Frame Film-making with
Puppets and Models
Second edition
pages cm
ISBN 978-1-4725-2190-3 (pbk.)
ISBN 978-1-4725-3943-4 (epdf)
1. Stop-motion animation films.
I. Title.
TR897.6.P87 2014
777'.7--dc23
2013036010

Layout by Jane Harper
www.harperandcole.co.uk
Printed and bound in China

Cover image:
The Maker, directed by Christopher Kezelos
www.themakerfilm.com
Image courtesy of Zealous Creative

0.1

Recipe 2013

director and animator
Andreas de Ridder
A hand and a puppet – the
raw materials, shown in this
commercial from Loose Moose,
produced by Glenn Holberton
for Unilever Brands DNA.

6   Foreword

8   Introduction

12   What is stop-motion?

14   The beginnings

18   The illusion of movement

26   Physicality

32   A continuous
     performance

36   Special effects

44   Wholly animated films

47   A one-minute film:
     The story

48   Focusing the idea

50   Art and truth

52   Externalizing internal
     thoughts

56   Stories and themes

60   Them and us

62   Approaching the story

66   A change of perspective

72   Out of the mouths of...
     talking umbrellas?

80   Economics

89   A one-minute film:
     Who and where?

90   The puppets

92   Telling the story
     with puppets

94   The physical puppet

100 Telling characteristics

104 Stylized movement

106 Heads and replacements

110 Eyes

114 Hands

116 Puppet size

118 Clay

122 Other techniques

129 A one-minute film:
     Getting ready

130 Preparations

132 Working with others

134 Storyboards

136 Sets

144 Costume

148 Colour

151 A one-minute film:
Practical puppets

152 Tools and techniques

154 Practicalities

166 Lighting

170 Sound

176 Dialogue

180 On-set effects

183 Editing

187 A one-minute film:
Filming

**188 Movement and
performance**

190 Animating on the set

196 Puppet design
and movement

202 Helping the movement

208 Performance

213 A one-minute film:
Putting it together

214 Conclusion

216 A brief history of stop-motion

218 Index

226 Picture credits

228 Acknowledgements

Stop-motion animation combines the visual and dramatic language of the cinema with the fragile and poignant moment that occurs when an object, inherently dead, aspires to life – this aspiration is the backbone of puppetry.

As a practitioner of puppets in the theatre, I have experience only of the linear time of a live performance, without the stops of the animator, but have, since the beginning, drawn sustenance and inspiration from the world of stop-motion and the dignity this work has given to the task of the puppet. Puppetry, the using of an object that has no life to tell the story of living beings, carries a contradiction that is taken even further when this life, this motion of the puppet is created by constantly halting it at every fragmentary increment. Yet this very contradiction has the power to show life as it is never seen in the literal world of straight cinema, where people walk and talk, and dogs run, and birds fly effortlessly.

The very fact that the stop-motion figure has to strive for that life so taken for granted in the 'outside world' points us as viewers of the created life of stop-motion to the inherent fragility of life itself, its precious provisionality.

When a stop-motion figure lives, breathes and thinks, it is charming simply because it does.

I first saw this in high school watching a documentary on the great Czech animator Jiří Trnka. He was building a figure that would become a cowardly prince in a film on Czech legends. He lathed its simple head, painted its almost abstract, immobile features, attached it to an armature, which was then costumed. The prince was placed on a set, a dark passage at night in a palace, and frame by frame he was made to walk backwards. Trnka, already an elderly artist, moved the prince's body with infinite care between each picture. Then the documentary maker switched gear: through the lens of Trnka's camera these single frames were speeded up until the prince, clearly scared by something fearsome in front of him, which we couldn't see, was backing off down the passage, shafts of moonlight illuminating only parts of his body. His arm came up to shield his face as his foot stepped into a basin full of jewels, which clattered and echoed in the passage, and the prince stumbled backwards, terrified, into the darkness…

His face never moved, I have never seen the rest of the film, yet the truth of the scene is as vivid for me today as when I saw it 45 years ago. This fragment proved to me that a puppet had the power to tell the big stories.

Stop-motion Animation very clearly sets out the fundamentals of the form whilst simultaneously introducing the reader to its whole history, illustrating each step with the work of the artists who have made the industry what it is today. Reading it, then, is a double pleasure. You feel a beginner amongst expert colleagues.

Stop-motion animation

When struggling to focus an audience's attention on some small action in the constant 'wide shot' of the live theatre, it's possible to envy the arsenal of aides provided by a camera… close-ups, camera movements, camera angles, the cut…

But then there is a price to these luxuries.

The animator spends countless hours alone with a host of characters and the map of their movements held precariously in the mind as slowly, patiently, frame by frame, the drama of life in the world is wrought into movement.

Adrian Kohler
Artistic Director, Handspring Puppet Company

There is no right or wrong way to make animated films – and no particular animation technique that is superior to all the rest. Our job, if we choose to work in this wonderfully bizarre medium, is to communicate something to an audience, and to keep them entertained and interested, all the while ensuring that the technique is appropriate to the subject. The technique that we're concerned with in this book is stop-motion – so, what is stop-motion?

Today an exact answer is bound to be somewhat imprecise, as most animation techniques contain elements and principles that overlap. Stop-motion could be generally defined as manipulating, between sequentially exposed frames of film or video, usually directly by hand, some tangible object, whether it be a complex puppet, a paper cut-out, sand, a discarded piece of junk or furniture. When played back, the object gives the appearance of movement, performance and independent life, though this 'life' is 'lifeless' – an illusion. The motion is created when the camera is stopped: a wonderful oxymoron, and it's easy to see how this glorious craft gets its name.

If any of this excites you, let's go.

0.2

Other animation techniques follow the same process but with a succession of drawings or computer-generated (CG) images. Again, movement is created when the camera is stopped. A frame shows no actual movement. This could apply to all film – the image is projected for a fraction of a second, and after a black frame, is replaced by a subsequent image. If the images relate to each other enough, the brain assumes there is continuous movement. If the consecutive images are too different the brain struggles to make any connection.

0.2

Sleight of Hand: A Story in Stop-motion 2012

director
Michael Cusack
A creator contemplates his unusually full-scale creation before giving it life through stop-motion.

Producing 24–25 images for a second of film makes stop-motion a slow and truly laborious process, and even a short film demands huge resources, patience and unflagging energy. However, new technologies, such as smartphone apps, are making the resources more accessible and students are certainly still eager to work in this oldest of mediums.

Any animation exhibition will see the physical models drawing the crowds, with the public instinctively reaching out to touch. We cannot help ourselves. That these characters exist is one of the main satisfactions, and the intrigue of an inanimate object 'magically' moving by itself is never likely to lose its appeal.

Most audiences are savvy enough to tell whether what they are watching started life in a computer, or on paper, or as a solid object. This is not just due to the telltale marks in the sculpting, nor the texture and fabrics, but more due to the distinct movement. A puppet will always look like a puppet, and that's as it should be. The awareness of the technique, the trick, is very much part of the enjoyment.

Stop-motion is not the slickest or the smoothest of animation (CG claims that credit). It can't be, but this is part of the appeal of stop-motion. For every *Frankenweenie* (2012), which uses amazingly sophisticated puppets and animation, there is a film made with household objects, or lumps of clay. Both are valid approaches. What some see as failings, others see as joys, loving its quirkiness; the certain roughness, suggesting a human hand has been intimately and directly involved in a craft.

I love the trick of a physical object moving by itself in real space, and watching the unexpected and spontaneous ways the light interacts over the materials. I love an object being given an apparent life and the emotional resonances that brings. I love the trick. I love that I know it is a puppet. There is something shamanistic about stop-motion, as well as being suggestive of childhood games, which evokes deeper mythologies of giving life – such as the Frankenstein, Pygmalion and Golem stories. It is, of course, parental. The physicality of stop-motion makes all these concepts accessible, and that physicality is to be treasured, and not denied.

We will explore these particular qualities of stop-motion so that your film really does exploit all that is good and glorious about this special film-making technique, with particular reference to the more narrative and figurative or puppet-led films. We'll also explore how other disciplines tell their stories; other forms of puppetry and other mediums that share with stop-motion a joyous celebration of artifice.

By the time we finish you'll be eager and equipped to get started, and will be convinced that stop-motion is right for your film. Hopefully, you'll enjoy it as so many of us continue to do: it's not going away!

Stop-motion animation

0.3

0.3

Toby's Travelling Circus 2012–

director
Barry JC Purves
producers
**Richard Randolph
and Chris Bowden**
The characters of *Toby's
Travelling Circus* – a Mackinnon &
Saunders production for Komixx
and Channel 5. Photograph by
Dick Dando.

1.1

To start, we will look at how stop-motion evolved, almost by accident, in the early days of cinema. We'll look at what it is as well as how it works and its pros and cons. We'll explore the uniquely tactile technique of stop-motion; how this differs from other animation methods and why the process is part of its appeal. We'll see the many different ways it has been used over the years and how the accessibility of recent technological developments is affecting it.

Finally, we'll look at how best to use this technique for your own film.

1.1

Oh Willy... 2012

directors
**Emma De Swaef and
Marc James Roels**
Emma De Swaef on the set
of *Oh Willy...*

In late nineteenth-century Paris, Georges Méliès used invisible wires, trap doors, sheets of glass, smoke and complex automata to become a master of spectacular theatrical illusion and magic. Nearby, in Le Théâtre du Grand-Guignol (the theatre of the big puppet), young ladies were being decapitated and sawn in half twice nightly. Méliès' own productions were playful and whimsical, and his acts involved projecting films on stage, with characters walking from the stage into the film. Even then, he flirted with an awareness of the technique, crossing its apparent limitations. On one legendary occasion, Méliès was filming in the street when his camera jammed for a few seconds. This simple accident changed everything, for him and for us; the jump cut on the developed film had seemingly transformed, through a well-timed substitution, an omnibus into a hearse – a delicious deceit not lost on Méliès. The trick was merely using a technique from his stage illusions, where, with a wave of a cloth – that essential moment of misdirection – an actress dropped through a trap door to be instantly replaced by a skeleton. His camera glitch had created a magical illusion through the camera stopping – through stopping motion.

Visual tricks

This basic technique, of a trick happening unseen, still forms the basis of all stop-motion today. Modern technology can refine, multiply, clean, adapt the footage and smooth the joins, but we are still, unseen by the audience, repositioning a physical object, taking a frame, and then moving, replacing or removing it.

Méliès built a studio to cope with his special effects, which included disembodied heads made to grow and shrink and float. For this, he filmed actors partially wrapped in black velvet, against a black background, with only the relevant body parts registering on film. This is essentially how the ubiquitous green screen techniques work today. Green screen allows separate elements to be inserted into other pieces of film.

Over in St Albans in England, Arthur Melbourne-Cooper was also experimenting with stop-motion. In *A Dream of Toyland* (1907) and *Noah's Ark* (1908) he animated toys and wooden dolls. He can claim two other cinematic firsts – the first use of a close-up, an eye looking through a keyhole, and in *Matches: An Appeal (1899)* he used animated matches for a commercial.

Whilst Méliès' contemporaries, the Lumière Brothers, were recording everyday events, Méliès was thrusting his films into absolute fantasy. He used themes of devils, history, fairy tales and space travel, though sometimes he recreated real-world scenes the cameras missed – such as the coronation of Edward VII. He also used his fantasy techniques to sell commercial products – bringing fruit and vegetables to life is something all animators inevitably experience. His inventiveness and problem solving were astonishing, and he embodied the inquisitive quality that we all need.

What is stop-motion?

1.2

1.2

L'homme à la tête en caoutchouc 1901

animator
Georges Méliès
Georges Méliès achieving the impossible in *L'homme à la tête en caoutchouc* (*The Man with the Rubber Head*). His own disembodied head floats in front of him, achieved through a technique not unlike the green screen technique that is so common in modern films.

1.3

Animators are confronted with daily challenges as to how to achieve certain illusions. Aptly, Méliès was a magician, an outrageous performer, and a showman, and as a stop-motion animator you are all those. Stop-motion isn't about mathematics and facts and figures, but it is certainly about performance, tricks, illusions and instincts. Méliès only occasionally used pure stop-motion, as in *Cinderella* (1899), but he used it as a means of achieving his imaginative visions. He may not have invented stop-motion as we know it, but he certainly breathed it into glorious life.

All animators owe an enormous debt to Méliès' giddy fantasy films and to his joy of mixing theatre, film and animation techniques. It was good to see this debt celebrated in Martin Scorsese's *Hugo* (2011), where several films and Méliès' own studios are reconstructed in astonishing detail.

1.3

**The Story of the Fox
(Le roman de Renard)** 1930

director
Władysław Starewicz
These exquisite and surprisingly expressive puppets were some of the first to give creditable performances.

What is stop-motion?

Other early animators

Méliès didn't appear, like one of his tricks, out of nowhere. His work evolved out of decades, maybe centuries, of worldwide experiments with optical toys, and then the new film cameras and advances in technology – all driven by the common, deeply instilled need to give images life. Significant contemporaries included Edwin S. Porter in America, who used stop-motion to bring beds to life in the wonderful *Dream of a Rarebit Fiend* (1906). A year later J. Stuart Blackton animated objects to suggest supernatural activity, another recurring theme, in *The Haunted Hotel* (1907) while Émile Cohl had fun with dancing matches in *Bewitched Matches* (1913).

These films all used stop-motion as a consciously special 'special' effect, often within a live action context, but the pure manipulation of puppets, in a completely animated world, flourished with the amazing animal- and insect-led stories of Władysław Starewicz, such as *The Story of the Fox* (1930), and the charming *The Mascot* (1934). These films contain extraordinarily sophisticated and complex animation, with detailed puppets, which appeared to breathe. These characters are, without a doubt, performing and we can see their thought processes.

In 1933, having given life to model dinosaurs in *The Lost World* (1925), Willis H. O'Brien was faced with the challenge of showing a 30-foot ape rampaging through New York. Men in fur suits and trained animals were considered, but inserting an impressive stop-motion creation into live-action footage was the solution. Who knows? Had CG been available, would O'Brien have used it? Even today, O'Brien's technical achievement silences the harshest critics, but it is the psychological details and complex character of Kong that still touch us. After Kong kills a T-Rex in a brutal fight, he flicks the slack jaw of the dinosaur, as if making sure he has killed it. The unexpected moment of self-doubt still surprises and satisfies. Suddenly, among all the violence, there is a tender piece of character performance. There is a thought process and a 'special effect' becomes a performance. It is such an iconic moment that it was referenced in the 2005 version of the film.

After Starewicz's characters and O'Brien's tragic hero there was no doubt that animated characters could act and show psychological depth, and that's definitely part of our job.

That a succession of frames can create an illusion of continuous movement has been, in the past, attributed to a theory called 'persistence of vision'.

Many animators and film-makers understand this idea as a phenomenon whereby the human eye (with the brain) retains the images for a fraction of a second. The theory is that everything we perceive is a combination of what is happening right now and what happened an instant before, providing a fluid link between successive images. Film-making, and especially animation, depends on the brain to link these separate images. Scientists and psychologists still argue over the theory and precisely how we formulate movement, but what is essential to animators is to help the brain and eye to construct the movement between frames. We can do this by relating each frame to the ones either side as much as possible. If we make the animation increments too large from one frame to another, there is simply not enough information for the brain to find a link and the movement falls to pieces.

1.4

Pas de deux 1968

animator
Norman McLaren
Norman McLaren's groundbreaking film *Pas de deux*, uses many consecutive images of a dancer in motion condensed into a single frame. The validity of the 'persistence of vision' theory is something of a minefield and is usually dismissed these days. It's suggested that if the theory was correct we would see movement like this image.

1.5

The Chimp Project 2001

producer
Handspring Puppet Company
photographer
Ruphin Coudyzer
A lively still from *The Chimp Project* directed by Adrian Kohler and Kurt Wustmann, with the puppeteers defiantly part of the action.

What is stop-motion?

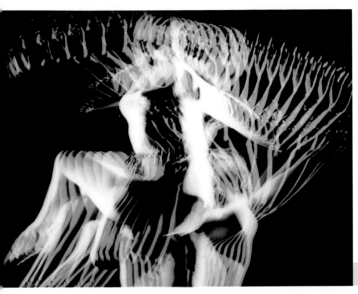

1.4

1.5

Continuous movement

In stop-motion, as with all animation, the successful creation of continuous movement depends on how one frame, or one position, relates to the previous and subsequent frames. The more a frame connects to the previous one, in terms not just of pose but also of colour, composition, exposure, framing and sound, the better and more credible the flow of the animation.

If two sequential frames have no relation to each other, the viewer's brain will struggle to make sense of the information being presented. The viewer will certainly not perceive any illusion of smooth movement. If in the first frame an object is positioned extreme left of frame, and in the second frame, it has been moved a bit to the right, then the viewer can quickly and easily make the assumption that the object has indeed moved to the right. There is the subconscious assumption that the object has taken the most direct path between the two positions. It's even better if the second position still overlaps the first position as there is a definite link. However, if the second frame showed the object at the extreme right, there is simply not enough information to fill in the huge gap. There is no link between the two positions, and the sequence won't read as movement.

If we want to create the illusion that the object has curved from the left of frame to the top centre of frame, and then down to the right, we are going to need more frames to describe this arc. A zigzagging movement will need even more detail to spell out the movement. Usually, there are 24 or 25 frames to a second of film, and the more complicated movements are going to need every one of those frames. The more detailed the movement, the more frames will be required. There are plenty of tricks to help. In live action, a moving object leaves a trailing blur on a frame of film, which helps suggest the direction of movement. Whoosh lines on cartoons have a similar effect, as do 'go faster' stripes on cars. In stop-motion, we don't usually have the luxury to blur the image, but we can give characters props or costume details, such as scarves that will trail behind, suggesting the direction of the movement. The way the environment reacts will help – leaves blowing in the wake of a moving object will also suggest not just the direction of movement but also the speed.

So, basically, we need to spell out each step of the movement. It is certainly not through reproducing real life but by over-emphasizing elements that help suggest the movement. Animation, by its very nature, cannot be realistic and nor should it be.

Of course, some movement may be intentionally fragmented and disconnected, but in general most movement will need some coherence, gained by relating each frame to the next.

Helping the eye read animation

The smoothness, or otherwise, of your animation depends on how much connected detail and information you can put into it.

In everyday life there's often excessive information that cannot be processed. Too much unconnected detail caused by rapid head movements, too much bobbing up and down or a lack of focus can all lead to disorientation and dizziness, often alleviated by just closing the eyes. Most people will blink at the start of a quick head turn to avoid having to deal with too much information on a move that looks like a **whip pan**. People on a roller coaster will be travelling too fast to make sense of what is rushing by, and will feel disorientated (or worse), though that's sometimes part of the appeal. Focusing on the static handrail or horizon can help focus the brain and prevent it overloading.

Similarly, if there is a wild and frantic piece of animation it helps to counterbalance this with a gentle, more controlled piece of movement elsewhere in the frame. This is no different to playing the piano. The right hand usually does all the more lively parts, while the left hand plods along lending a solid grounding to the piece. Take away the beat of the left hand and the right hand seems less focused.

Exercise: Puppetry

Stop-motion combines the relatively modern world of film with the ancient tradition of puppetry. Stop-motion is different from most other forms of puppetry as it is not performed or filmed in real time, nor is it played in front of an audience and, unusually for puppets, the operators are not seen.

Find as many different examples of puppetry as possible and see how the various techniques help or hinder the character's movement. See how the technique is used in the storytelling.

Whip pan is when a camera moves from one position to another at such a speed that the viewer hardly registers what is between the two positions.

A static counterpoint

Often, to let a movement work, the animation needs a static component – a lovely contradiction. If an animated character were moving against a blank background in flat lighting, the effect of the actual movement would not read as well as if there were light and shade, or dappled lighting and a background with detail. This movement registers by contrasting against something that is not moving. This particularly applies to stop-motion, where characters are moving in a real space. Conversely, imagine having a camera move following an object against a blank background and with uniform lighting; how are we to know it is actually travelling? A detailed background or textured lighting informs the movement. In my films, the characters often perform against black backgrounds, but we make sure that the textured lighting embroiders the movement. My own film *Plume* (2011) saw the character spend time sprawled out on black velvet. We could have gently crept the camera in on him as he lay prone, but with no detail in the background he would have appeared to have been sliding about.

It is important to focus on the movement, making it easy for the viewer's eyes and brain to perceive what's important, even if it means over-emphasizing the storytelling moments and the mechanics of the movement. If the animation includes too many quick cuts or overly large or small movements, it just won't '**read**' properly to the viewer. If a movement does not read, we are rather wasting our time.

Read, here, means to understand or register the meaning or significance of what is seen.

1.6

1.6

Achilles 1996

director
Barry JC Purves
Here, a strong pose emphasizing
the storytelling moments of
a movement is helped by a
trailing tail that gives the illusion
of momentum and inertia. Our
animation is all about illusion not
accurate reproduction.

Transcending realism

Animation techniques such as 2D drawings, working with clay, and CG images can all suggest the weight and inertia of a movement through squashing and stretching a character. However, this is trickier with solid puppets, and means we need to find other ways and tricks to show the weight and size of a character. We'll come to these, but it is worth noticing that having to over-emphasize points in an action starts to take the movement, certainly stop-motion movement, away from merely reproducing live action. Instead, it becomes a more stylized movement, and this is to be encouraged and enjoyed.

What works for live action does not necessarily work for stop-motion and this requires a different approach. This is actually a surprising liberation. You'll find that even the most mannered movement can still contain a truth. If you have the sensibilities of a dancer, a mime, or an actor, all of whom thrive on a movement that is more about storytelling and emotion than reality, then you are likely to find stop-motion a real pleasure.

1.7

The Man Who Was Afraid of Falling 2011

writer and director
Joseph Wallace
In this film, rather than copying real life through invisible technique, the joy of the illusion and the artifice is magnificently on display.

1.8

Next 1989

director
Barry JC Purves
The dangling, trailing arms and hanging head of the dummy suggest weight in a puppet that weighed little. It is best to show the laws of physics at work even in a fantastical scene. Everything needs its own conventions. Photograph by Dave Alex Riddett.

1.7

1.8

One of the main attractions of stop-motion is that the animator is handling something very physical that is moving and existing in a tangible space, reacting with spontaneity to light and focus and depth. In other forms of animation, shadows have to be added, but in a well-lit stop-motion, shadows happen naturally and give an absolutely credible existence to the characters. The puppet is directly connected to its world, which can only help the believability of its narrative. Much effort is spent with CG animation and cel animation making sure that the characters are in direct contact with the ground, and too often they can look as if they are sliding or in a different plane. With stop-motion this is not an issue as the characters are actually there on set casting real shadows.

1.9

Bobby Yeah 2011

writer, director, producer
Robert Morgan
Robert Morgan's *Bobby Yeah* is full of wonderfully unsettling textures.

Texture and lighting

With physical characters comes texture, another great asset of stop-motion, and we can make the most of it with effective lighting. There's little point in sculpting a gloriously detailed puppet, or sets, costumes or backgrounds, then flattening out all the textures with very dull uniform front lighting. The character would then start to look like a cartoon. In low-budget or lazy cartoons characters are often not affected by lighting or the background geography. As a consequence, the characters pass through their environment without causing shadows or any other physical sign of connecting with the world around them. Start to imagine the narrative possibilities that shadows, texture and atmosphere can bring to a story.

That said, however, CG animation is now capable of producing extraordinarily realistic textures on its characters. CG can give its animal characters beautiful fur with the suggestion of muscles underneath that stop-motion can't even contemplate. These shadows and textures are possible as a result of many decisions, vast effort and much coordinating between the riggers who build the virtual armatures, and the texture and lighting artists. With stop-motion, put the puppets in a lit space and you're halfway there. Stop-motion animators can enjoy the fact that once the puppets have been sculpted, all the effort of making them look connected to their world happens for free. As we'll see, there are also a variety of little tricks to further secure a character in their world.

What is stop-motion?

1.9

Detail

The detail possible on puppets often surprises audiences. This is an enjoyable element of the craft that we should relish. Small details help provide additional information about the intended scale of the figures and sets, giving the characters a history and personality, locating them in a credible world. We are, after all, trying to make characters that are in reality only a few inches tall, appear to be much bigger. We have to be careful that ill-chosen fabrics or props or textures do not counteract the illusion. However, many animators are very happy to remind the audience that they are, in fact, looking at small objects and yet are being moved by them. That is another joy of stop-motion – a puppet will always be a puppet, but that seldom stops us believing in it.

Including detail in drawn animation can be frustrating and extremely labour intensive – although not impossible. Imagine having to reproduce every bristling hair of an animal or the swirls of a brocaded dress in every frame.

To some extent, drawn animation works by capturing as much as possible with as little as possible, making every line and detail reveal something. Actually, that would be a good suggestion for all animation. Only include a line, a detail, and a gesture if it can contribute.

1.10

1.10

Lost and Found 2012

animator
Joan C. Gratz
Joan Gratz developed the
technique known as clay painting.
This involves animating clay,
blending colours to create a
seamless flow of images. In this
short film, *Lost and Found*, we
see a haunting face animated in
clay, lit to make the most of the
texture and relief.

What is stop-motion?

Some drawn animation contains an inordinate amount of detail, but the sheer effort and control of reproducing such complexity can lead to inaccuracy in the lines. This inaccuracy gives the lines a life of their own. This is not necessarily a good thing, if a clean and precise effect is wanted, but in work such as the vibrant, lively films of Joanna Quinn, her lines positively dance with joy, celebrating the pencil that drew them. The nearest we have to this energy in stop-motion is clay animation when the animator is quite loose and spirited with the sculpting, and enjoys the flexible random qualities of the material. Most animators are content to leave fingerprints in the clay, again happily announcing the technique. Clay is unlikely ever to produce realistic animation, but that is not the point. We should be relishing the artifice – a theme I keep returning to.

1.11

1.11

Wife of Bath 1998

animator
Joanna Quinn
Joanna Quinn's gloriously fleshly *Wife of Bath* film uses a lively and spontaneous line – the human hand is very evident in the technique. The movement in the line gives the characters much energy; in effect giving them life. The detail in the characters also separates them easily from the looser, less important backgrounds.

1.12

1.12

The Curse of the Were-Rabbit
2005

directors
Nick Park and Steve Box
Wallace, Gromit and Lady
Tottington enjoying the
exaggerated features, textures
and material that define their
characters. Strong, clean
shapes in clay and Plasticine
are easier to maintain during the
constant resculpting than more
detailed characters.

Recommended viewing

Do watch Garri Bardin's *Grey Wolf
and Little Red Riding Hood* (1990).
The sculpting does not have the
finesse of Gromit, but it does have a
mad energy that suits its kinetic form
of storytelling. The resculpting is a
conscious feature in its own right.
Similarly, in Adam Elliot's sensitive
films, some of the joy is in seeing the
manipulation of the Plasticine itself.
Adam's animation works, ironically,
by how little it moves – take a look at
his remarkable films *Harvie Krumpet*
(2003) and *Mary and Max* (2009) to
see how effective this is.

What is stop-motion?

Clay faces

Animators working with puppets are lucky that once a face has been sculpted, the detail is there for good. However, if you are working with Plasticine or clay, a face still requires a lot of work to maintain. Should you sculpt a character whose face is full of interesting wrinkles it will be extremely hard to keep these wrinkles consistent, not just through the constant handling of the soft material but through re-sculpting so much detail in most frames. It's easy for the face to evolve unnecessarily during a shot. Clay is different from other forms of stop-motion as it generally involves re-sculpting as well as animating each exposure. The material is easily marked, and the continual smoothing out can certainly eat into the shooting schedule. Having animation skills for clay is essential but useless without also possessing the skills of a sculptor.

Much of the immense attraction of clay animation is that the audience is aware that the characters are clay, and yet they are totally drawn into their story. The material inevitably leads to a glorious chunkiness and heaviness in the animation – if you choose to work with clay, make sure that this effect is appropriate to your subject. This chunkiness seldom prohibits a good performance, and clay is great if you want to give your characters a 'stretch and squash' fluid anatomy.

Watch one of Aardman's *Wallace and Gromit* films or one of Adam Elliot's beautiful clay character studies, and see how much the figures emote and communicate. Gromit, in particular, is designed around strong, clean shapes, that are easy to maintain from frame to frame but is still capable of tremendous nuances. Expression comes not just from his eyes and gently raised eyebrows, but also wonderfully varied timing and knowing glances. Watch, Elliot's characters' beautifully timed blinks. Blinking is such an effective way of seeing the thought process, and sometimes this is all that is needed. A real case of less is more. Clay animation is a time-consuming process and you need to make sure that every movement is controlled and says something.

Of course, there's no rule to say that the whole figure has to be sculpted of clay. You can just use clay for the most flexible features, such as the mouth, within a more permanent face. Also, filming time can be saved by having pre-sculpted replacement shapes that slot in.

Don't be put off by how labour-intensive working with clay is. You can simply grab a lump of clay now, load a stop-motion app into your phone, and off you go, with fun and immediate results, morphing shape after shape.

Most animation goes through several processes, with different elements being animated at different times, or by setting the key positions first, and then filling in with in-betweens. Stop-motion has none of that, and works with a direct, intimate through line. You literally start at frame one of a shot, and finish with the last frame, organically shaping the shot as you go. This linear, straight-ahead form of shooting helps the action develop and flow. It is also a very satisfying and logical way to film. It is a continuous performance in small chunks and, assuming you are the only animator touching the puppet, this leads to strong continuity in the performance.

Personality transfer

With this intimacy between puppet and animator certain characteristics of either can be transferred. With a puppet in his hand, the animator will get the most direct and honest response in the animation. There's no technology, no one else to get in the way. This can occasionally be a drawback, with the animator's personality colouring the animation too much, especially on a major project where a role will be shared by several animators. Mostly, though, it is a benefit and animators are often cast for scenes based on their strengths. Some find slapstick scenes easier, while others cope better with more emotional scenes. It would be a shame, though, not to let the personality of the animator emerge through the puppet.

As with other puppetry, it is important to revel in the direct contact between puppet and puppeteer. The contact between a human hand and the puppet gives the animation so much 'soul', to use a clichéd word.

1.13

Sleight of Hand: A Story in Stop-motion 2012

director
Michael Cusack
The animator's hand is uniquely visible in this short, raising all manner of ideas about the awareness of the process.

1.14

Billy Twinkle: Requiem for a Golden Boy 2012

puppeteer
Ronnie Burkett
Master puppeteer Ronnie Burkett is defiantly visible as he operates his many puppets. It is often the unpredictability of the human interaction with a physical object that gives the characters so much spirit.

Animating live

Most stop-motion animators and audiences enjoy its quirkiness, its physicality and its little imperfections. Similarly, most animators enjoy the fact that you don't generally, certainly not when shooting on film, get the chance to refine. Once you have repositioned a character, you have immediately lost the previous frame. It may be recorded on a playback system, but the real move has gone. This is both a huge pressure and also part of the excitement.

You can have a performance planned out in your mind's eye, but I guarantee that the puppet will do something else, or you will time a move differently, and with no chance of starting again, you simply have to work with the shot. This is as near to acting in front of a live audience, with all the adrenalin that that implies, as it is possible to get in animation. It can make you feel naked, frustrated, excited, vulnerable and exposed. How you react to that pressure must colour how you feel about stop-motion. Shooting on digital has eased this pressure somewhat, as there is no tense waiting for rushes, and as you watch the shot build up frame by frame you can feel if it is working, or quickly abort if the puppet has missed a mark. Shooting blind, without playback, was certainly exciting, even if the work lacked the finesse possible now.

Although your first short film might be achieved largely alone, at college, or at home with your iPhone and animation app, on large projects you will most certainly be part of a team. Most of a stop-motion crew tend to be in the same studio space; this is unlike CG animation where much of the work is fragmented and farmed out overseas, or to other studios, and a central Internet base used to view the progress. Stop-motion, by its nature, cannot be farmed out as all the puppets, sets and crew need to be together. This creates a tight group with camaraderie, and tensions, but you are constantly reminded of being part of a team. The CG studios try hard to engender these group dynamics with shared meetings and discussions and activities, but on an hour-by-hour basis other animation is not as tight-knit as stop-motion. A collective, contributive team spirit is important to feeling part of a project, and hugely satisfying. I enjoy being part of a team, all heading in the same direction – some may find this brings extra pressures. It's not usually practical to be a one-man team with stop-motion.

What is stop-motion?

1.15

1.15

I Am Tom Moody 2012

director and writer
Ainslie Henderson
Ainslie Henderson animating his award-winning film *I Am Tom Moody.* In a film about alter egos, it is no coincidence that Ainslie is wearing an almost identical sweater to his character.

Stop-motion is now most often used as a medium in its own right, and that's what concerns us in this book. However, many of the techniques used in purely animated films were developed over the years in which the technique was used as a special effect within live-action films, when certain ideas simply couldn't be achieved any other way.

1.16

King Kong 1933

animator
Willis H. O'Brien
In 1933, stop-motion was the most practical way to bring this fantasy creature to life. It allowed Kong to perform and thereby allowed the audience to truly engage with him as a character alongside the human actors in the film.

A practical solution

King Kong (1933), Willis H. O'Brien's most famous creation, was a mere 45cm (18 inches) tall but was pretending to be the size of a house. Stop-motion was used to create the illusion of this enormous beast as other suggested methods simply were not convincing enough. Stop-motion allowed Kong to be performed with great controlled nuances, and with a compelling physicality. At the time, stop-motion was the best possible technique for bringing a fantasy creature to life on the big screen. However, in Peter Jackson's 2005 re-imagining of the story a motion-capture performance was entirely appropriate, and led to a performance that was more physical, more intimate and more appropriate to the dynamic tone of the film.

Modern audiences would be unlikely to accept the distinct movement of stop-motion in such a visceral and kinetic live-action film. The use of camera moves is another major contrast between the two performances. O'Brien gives the effect of a moving camera, but was seldom able to actually move the camera itself in the animation scenes. CG, with its virtual camera, has seen the camera, both in terms of its movement and where it can go, become utterly liberated. Remember, when approaching your film, the limitations a physical camera imposes on the process.

1.17

King Kong 2005

animator
Weta Digital
By 2005, technology and
audience expectations had
both moved on. This meant that
Andy Serkis' motion capture
performance and Weta Digital
3D animation were a far more
suitable choice to make the
modern-day Kong believable.

Stop-motion stunt work

Stop-motion has also pretended to be live action in stunts too dangerous for the actors to perform – or when the logistics were just too complicated and expensive to do it for real. A short, almost invisible shot in *The Adventures of Baron Munchausen* (1988) has a puppet of John Neville sat astride a huge cannonball flying through the air, much as there had been puppets of Fay Wray in the 1933 *King Kong*. Similarly, the exhilarating animated runaway mine cart sequences in *Indiana Jones and the Temple of Doom* (1984) obviously saved on the building of a huge set. This sequence used many hi-tech tricks to try to make the stop-motion indistinguishable from the live action. In the same film, the lowering of a puppet of Kate Capshaw into a fiery pit saved the actress certain discomfort, and the need to build a deep pit. However, because of stop-motion's quirkiness and the sophistication of CG, such sequences now look slightly awkward when cut directly next to the live action.

Many early films used stop-motion puppets for characters in unusual situations, such as Buster Keaton on a dinosaur in *Three Ages* (1923), but the technique was also used in combination with model sets of fantasy landscapes, or sets that could not be built full-scale in a studio. Across these sets – often further enhanced by beautiful matte paintings of castles or dramatic scenery – live-action model trains stutter or stop-motion vehicles crash, usually with a very static human character inside. Interestingly, there's an equivalent analogy to this today where stop-motion worlds are supplemented by CG elements to create a scale of landscape or weather conditions not possible in a limited studio space and schedule. In the past, stop-motion, and model work, often took over when live action could not achieve something, and now CG takes over when model work can't achieve a certain effect.

In old horror films you'll find stop-motion killer tree vines or skeletons dissolving or even coming back to life layer by layer through time lapse or stop-motion. It does pop up in surprising places. Hitchcock's early films are full of miniature work, and who knows how he might have achieved his proposed film of 'The Food of the Gods'. To a modern audience these scenes of stop-motion and models spliced into live-action films or masquerading as live action simply look uncomfortable, with the scale betrayed all too easily through a different feel to the focus, or the lighting or the movement. Elements such as fire, water and smoke notoriously look unconvincing when used with miniature models. The water droplets are simply too big and do not behave the same way as large expanses of water. This is where CG imagery has superseded stop-motion. It can make these effects utterly convincing. Stop-motion would have to be used with some irony to work next to live-action today, such as the appearance of the homunculus in *The League of Gentlemen's Apocalypse* (2005) and the remarkable animated hedgehog sequence in the otherwise live-action feature *A Fantastic Fear of Everything* (2012).

What is stop-motion?

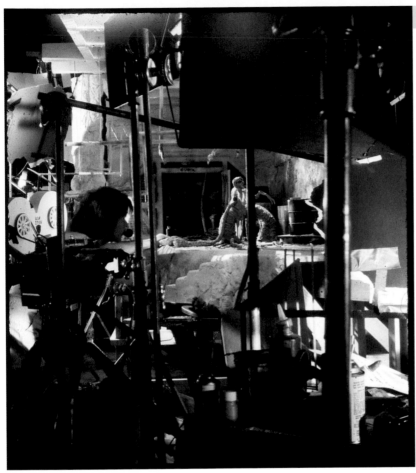

1.18

1.18

The Thing 1982

director
John Carpenter
The multi-Oscar-winning
Randall William Cook at work,
with characteristic pipe, on an
impressive stop-motion insert
sadly cut from John Carpenter's
live-action *The Thing*.

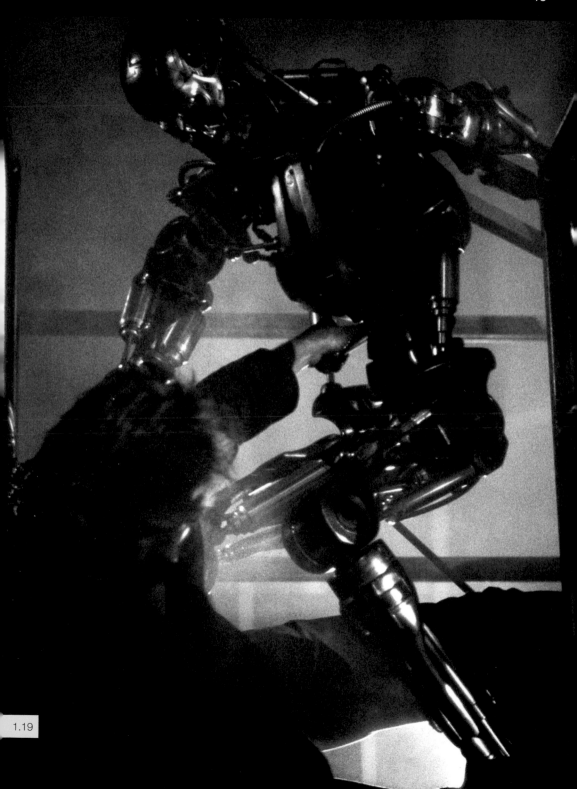

1.19

Futuristic machinery

The AT-AT walkers in *The Empire Strikes Back* (1980) were stop-motion models on miniature sets filmed to look like huge machines. Today they would almost certainly be created as CG models, with much more control and finesse (although an army of fans would miss their pleasingly distinctive walk and the fact they did actually exist as models). These AT-AT machines, like the two-legged ED-209 stop-motion model in *RoboCop* (1987), some of the underwater vehicles in *The Abyss* (1989), and the legendary shots in *The Terminator* (1984), were trying to be realistic and convincingly integrated into an otherwise live-action film. There was no other way to create such illusions. Real full-scale models could have been built and controlled with miles of cables, but the cost would have been prohibitive. Stop-motion models were a practical answer – the human hand doing away with the need for complex machinery.

In films such as *Earth vs. the Flying Saucers* (1956) the saucers were stop-motion creations and the technique was taken further in *batteries not included* (1987), where the main characters of small flying saucers were performed through a combination of stop-motion models against green screen and live-action models on wires or rods. In this kind of film, if a miniature model needs a smoother movement than is usually possible with stop-motion, the model can sometimes be moved during the actual exposure of the frame through external rods attached to motors. This 'go-motion' technique leads to a blurring of the action, which creates a more fluid move than traditional stop-motion. Again, CG has squashed that.

1.19

The Terminator 1984

director
James Cameron
A seamless combination of life-sized, live-action animatronic puppets and miniature stop-motion puppets were used to create the original Terminator.

Bringing fantasy to life

The breathtakingly performed and much-loved dinosaurs and creatures of Jim Danforth, David W. Allen, Phil Tippett, Ray Harryhausen and Randall William Cook may not look, by comparison, as sophisticated or as complex as the CG imagery of films that began with *Jurassic Park* (1993), but this takes away none of the artistry. Digital technology allows every scale or ripple of muscles under the skin to be animated, even over-animated, and every hair can glisten with sweat – such effects are seldom achievable in stop-motion. CG makes it possible to achieve incredibly detailed anatomy and realistic movement, and suggesting the scale of these creatures is scarcely a problem.

In contrast, even the most sophisticated stop-motion is noticeable when placed alongside live action. There is something about the focus, the lighting, and especially the movement that betray their small scale. However, on most occasions we are very grateful for that. As a stop-motion Raquel Welch clings gamely from the claws of a pterodactyl in *One Million Years BC* (1966) most audiences do not for one moment forget the impressive technique needed for the illusion, but that does not hamper their enjoyment of the film. It often increases it.

Interestingly, Talos and the skeletons, from the sublime *Jason and the Argonauts* (1963), still take the breath away, as the stop-motion movement is highly appropriate for the fantastical figures of an awkward heavy statue and skeletons. Through no fault of the stunning animation, creatures such as Pegasus and Calibos from *Clash of the Titans* (1981) have fared less well. This is largely because the audience are now wise to the difference between live action

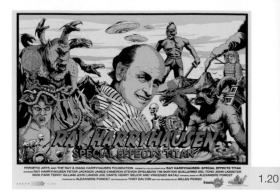

1.20

and stop-motion in consecutive shots. CG has made such a blend seamless. The stop-motion and sculpting are still hugely impressive but are comparably less credible when seen alongside live action and it is therefore understandable that the 2010 remake used CG to create the fantasy creatures. However, if you took the 1981 creatures and put them into a wholly model world their brilliance would be showcased. The achievement is even more dazzling when you consider the lack of video playback that is now deemed essential. So much relied on instinct; a quality that can be trampled by technology. Regardless of how advances in animation technology might colour the modern audience's perception of these films, the astonishing creations of Ray Harryhausen and friends remain stunning achievements and are, arguably, the most influential and most-loved animation ever. Their charm will never date. Thank goodness.

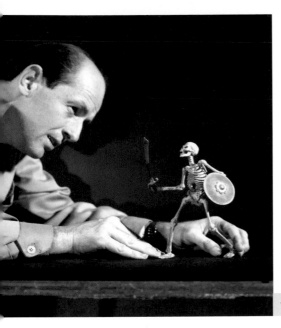

1.21

1.20

Ray Harryhausen: Special Effects Titan 2011

writer and director
Gilles Penso
Arguably the most influential and most loved of stop-motion animators. A poster for the feature film celebrating the extraordinary achievements of Ray Harryhausen.

The crux of the matter is that stop-motion is still an absolutely credible art form, with numerous wholly animated features in the last few years, and it fares best in its own environment (not when directly placed next to CG or live action). It still works for quirky creations and mechanical objects in a live-action setting, when the movement needs to be different, or with a suitable distancing or ironic devices such as dream characters, but it can no longer blend seamlessly with live-action footage. And that's fine. We should still enjoy stop-motion for all its quirks, when it is appropriate.

1.21

The 7th Voyage of Sinbad 1958

animator
Ray Harryhausen
director
Nathan Juran
Skeletons perfectly embody the most basic stop-motion notion of animating the inanimate, and there are three astonishing scenes in the films of Ray Harryhausen involving skeletons. This character was seen first in *The 7th Voyage of Sinbad*, and then in *Jason and the Argonauts* as one of seven skeletons. Another of this army later reappeared in *The First Men in the Moon*.

The most visible and celebratory use of stop-motion is in wholly animated films, when every prop, every costume, every character, every piece of set, have all been created in miniature scale. Every element of these films has the same design integrity. In wholly animated films, such as *$9.99* (2008), *Coraline* (2009), *Mary and Max*, *The Pirates! In an Adventure with Scientists!* (2012), *Frankenweenie*, *ParaNorman* (2012), *Selkirk, The Real Robinson Crusoe* (2012) and *Minhocas* (2013), the animation can really shine without the competition of live-action movement.

The unique movement and often heavily stylized and lit sets all complement and work together artfully. Suddenly, in an appropriate context, the animation does not look awkward or second rate or inferior to live action, but is seen as something fitting and wonderfully quirky. It seems likely that films like this will continue to be made for a long time, whatever the advances in computer technology. Films such as Wes Anderson's *Fantastic Mr. Fox* (2009) make direct reference to this quirkiness with sudden stops and starts, and with very self-conscious, theatrical sets. It is letting stop-motion be stop-motion, and exploiting its qualities. It is enjoying the artifice: an idea we must not lose.

Stop-motion no longer needs to compete with the sophistication of computers and can now enjoy being low-tech. Certainly, there have been some excellent but deliberately low-tech commercials and short films with little more than roughly animated cereals, or hundreds of Post-it notes or small toys or even chalk drawings or paintings on real walls, such as in the films by BLU. A recent music video, *Her Morning Elegance*, created the world of its female protagonist by merely using sheets, pillows and anything found in a bedroom. Here, an awareness of the technique, and the limitations, is essential. A complete feature film, *A Town Called Panic* (2009) used small plastic toys that were joyously shoved along, and in moments of relative luxury, replacement figures suggested different poses; and spring 2014 sees the much-awaited *Lego Movie*, using the collectable characters, gloriously celebrating their limited movement – both films are a complete antithesis to the uber-sophisticated techniques of *ParaNorman* but just as important. Seeing these films side by side is like watching *Finding Nemo* (2003) next to *South Park: Bigger, Longer & Uncut* (1999) – neither film is lesser for their technique. Most films relish their particular technique; audiences enjoy seeing and understanding the trick of animation, however limited or sophisticated.

1.22

1.22

The Pirates! In an Adventure with Scientists! (The Pirates! Band of Misfits) 2012

directors
Peter Lord and Jeff Newitt
The gloriously motley Plasticine and armatured crew from Aardman's *The Pirates!*

What people like about stop-motion animation is that it's real. It's like a magic trick; taking real things, real sets, and making them come to life with movement.
Joe Clokey

Real-world settings

Another technique is to place an entirely animated cast of characters into a real-world setting, and deliberately play on the artifice. Have a look at *Roof Sex* (2001) by Pes and *Britain* by Bexie Bush (2011), which both feature real furniture in outdoor settings behaving very tellingly. The joyously inventive and provocative short film, *I Live in the Woods* (2008), by Max Winston, had the central character, a 30cm (12-inch) puppet, running along real country roads, climbing trees, and interacting with the environment; no mattes were necessary as the character was there in the real world. The moving shadows and flickering light add to the already enormous energy of the film. The scale of the puppet, in the context of the film, is never an issue. This film echoes the inventive cult BBC series from the mid-1960s called *The Pogles*, which saw small animated puppets running around real woods. The makers of this series, Peter Firmin and Oliver Postgate, were also responsible for some wonderfully bizarre and much-loved stop-motion series, including *The Clangers* (1969–1974) and *Bagpuss* (1974).

1.23

1.23

I Live in the Woods 2008

animator
Max Winston
Here Max Winston animates his character in a real setting in a raw, provocative film bursting with energy.

The story

So let's make a one-minute film and, without any ado, let's get the story. Turn to page 6 of a newspaper and find the smallest article on it. Ignore the characters and settings for the moment, but look at the inherent drama.

Ask yourself:

- What dilemmas do the characters face? What is the conflict? How is it resolved?

- Is there anything unusual about it, anything that animation could enlighten and would animation tricks add anything to the story?

- If the incident is inherently dull, can you make it more interesting by telling the story in reverse, or from the viewpoint of a bystander who could have been affected by the event?

- Or did the journalist totally misinterpret the event?

- Is this event the end of the story? How did they get there?

- Whose point of view is the story told from?

Basically, what is the story? What is the conflict? Whose story is it? What journey do they go through? Ask yourself: What if? Limit yourself to one main character and one supporting character.

Now write it down in a three-act structure:

1 Setting up the situation

2 Complicating it

3 Resolving it, with a surprise coda that perhaps changes things or hints at something larger than the initial story

In the next chapter, we'll get to know your characters a little better...

In this chapter, we will look at how the particular and quite extraordinary qualities of stop-motion lend themselves perfectly to certain stories and characters but may look inappropriate when used in other contexts.

We'll also consider how to make the most of these qualities and start to enjoy what stop-motion can bring to a film, as opposed to disguising it as an invisible effect. Finally, we'll look at how the very physical and labour-intensive nature of stop-motion, and its budgets, can affect the storytelling.

2.1

A Christmas Dream 1946

director
Karel Zeman
In this classic film a young girl receives new presents for Christmas and immediately discards her old rag doll. Santa appears and makes her dream about the rejected doll coming to life for various adventures. Imaginative stories about dreams coming true and dolls springing to life are perfect for animation.

We've talked about how the technique of animation and particularly stop-motion works, but let's backtrack somewhat, and ask: What on earth is it? Why do so many people invest so much time and money in animation, and why do so many people derive so much pleasure from watching it?

We have to touch, albeit briefly, on several major ideas, such as: What is Art? A huge question there, but all music, writing, painting, film drama, dance, opera and so forth work by employing certain constructs – by enjoying a certain amount of artifice – and animation is certainly steeped in artifice.

Artifice

Music is still sound and silence but provokes an emotional response through playing with patterns, harmonies, and rhythms and repetitions and, well, structure. It is a consciously artificial construct of sound. Painting is an arrangement of colours and light within a frame – however naturalistic the treatment, the painting is still structured and presented within a frame or at least a formal shape. Anything that is put on stage or film, by its definition, cannot be realistic, and certainly the notion of characters talking plot and dishing out back story while playing to an invisible **fourth wall** or camera is very fake. Someone somewhere has made certain artistic choices about what the audience should see or should not see, as well as the unspoken contract of turning up at a specific location at a certain time. There is organization involved and someone has played with structure and edited reality.

The process of editing itself is a very unnatural process; our real lives do not jump from scene to scene and our eyes do not have a zoom function. Someone has provided a perspective. Handwriting is little more than black-and-white lines, but the arrangement of the lines, the patterns, the artifice, strike a chord of recognition in the viewer and something is understood and conveyed. Sometimes these patterns need

The **fourth wall** is the space that separates a performer or performance from an audience. It is the conceptual barrier between any fictional work and its viewers or readers.

to be learnt through experience, or through culture; sometimes they are understood instinctively, but all art relies on artificiality, and on something being presented to an audience. Something is put out, expressed, to be acknowledged and to provoke a response. This is painfully simplistic, but as you approach your film, do enjoy the fact that all art has a real sense of presentation and artifice about it. How are you presenting your film to the audience? How are you teasing them, revealing your story and characters bit by bit? I love that the word 'play' immediately suggests a knowing game and participation.

But none of this artifice need get in the way of what the art is about. Art can't be 'the truth', but its artifice can be truthful. Maybe art is highly edited, well-fashioned bits of truth, with all the irrelevant bits cut out. How much all this is embroidered is often down to taste and the medium itself, but animation, where everything is usually created from scratch, is certainly about highly honed presentation and artifice, and this should be seen as liberating.

A journey

Whilst stillness and silence are part of art, a dancer is not a dancer unless they move; the marks from a pen only become writing when they move somewhere; a sound won't be anything else unless it encompasses time; a sentence or a story can only exist if it progresses.

Everything has to have a journey, so as you start to think about your film, ask yourself: What is the journey? This journey is for the characters, the creator but especially for the audience. What have we all learnt that we did not know at the start? The answer to that is the fun part of storytelling.

Most stories are about ourselves; about sharing our experience or points of view. These can be cries for help, or shouts of anger, or a celebration of our lives, or declarations of love, or about wanting to leave a mark, or lessons on how to live our lives, or attempts to make sense of what we don't understand – whatever we are trying to communicate, we are often not particularly good at speaking directly and honestly. Most people find it more comfortable to talk about themselves through the safety of metaphor, allusion or fable. And let's be honest, it's more interesting to have our dilemmas discussed with a little more colour and drama. We may be reluctant to talk directly about ourselves, for reasons of gender, politics, culture and so on. These stories can be our voices, and the lives led by our characters are lives we would like to lead without inhibition or recrimination. To a major extent, our characters become our alter egos. It seldom matters how fanciful a story is as long as we can find something in the drama that relates to our own experience. How would we react in that situation?

Our job as storytellers is to find devices that externalize the internal thoughts and desires and fears of our characters. We can be so honest through a bit of artifice. A clown can be more outrageous through merely putting on a red nose; a ventriloquist can get away with anything if his puppet says it; a cross-dresser, a superhero, a teenager on the Internet, a portrait in the attic; a long list of such personalities are more comfortable living through an alter ego. Shakespeare's *Hamlet*, a play stuffed full of astonishing human

insight, is also a play crammed full of brave, artificial and theatrical devices that enable the audience to learn more about the characters. Ghosts speak information that only certain characters hear; fey fools prattle on with some wisdom; actors perform a play that succinctly echoes the main drama and relationships; letters arrive with new information; songs reveal more than speech; daringly theatrical soliloquys talk of the characters' emotional dilemmas; bouts of madness allow some extraordinary insights, whilst a mere skull becomes a catalyst for the externalizing of the most profound internal thoughts. All this artificiality does not get in the way of the human drama. It's tempting to equate Yorick's skull, surely the most resonant prop ever, with Mary Poppins' umbrella, or Pinocchio's Jiminy Cricket. In more recent examples, we saw Mel Gibson with a beaver glove puppet attached to his hand in *The Beaver* (2011), and Mark Wahlberg cohabiting with a straight-talking Teddy bear in *Ted* (2012). They are all companions, consciences and therapists. Does your script contain any such changes of perspective that reveal the internal thoughts of the characters?

2.2

Hamlet 1948

director
Laurence Olivier
Yorick's skull, to some extent a puppet, becomes the catalyst for some deeply profound thoughts by Shakespeare's *Hamlet* – portrayed here by Sir Laurence Olivier.

Confounding the norm

Added to artifice, and changes of perspective, is the idea of confounding the norm, or of transgressing our expectations. We respond to seeing limits first established, and then crossed. Much of art depends on this. We watch a dancer, and then are surprised when she bends back further than we thought possible. We're fascinated when a singer holds a note longer than we can; or when a street artist becomes a living statue; or when Cinderella's little kitchen is transformed into a spectacular ballroom before our eyes; or when the froth of a cappuccino seems to suggest the Virgin Mary's face; or when a street artist has painted a huge chasm on the ground; or when real time is played in slow motion or with time-lapse; or when a cloud resembles a train; or when we marvel that the sculpted figures of Ron Mueck are not just astonishingly lifelike but also just happen to be enormous; or when we see a painted hand looking like an eagle; or when Dorothy's Tin Man wants a heart; or when an athlete jumps higher than we thought possible; or when characters appear to fly, or when the dead come back to life, or when we enjoy the beauty of Seurat's *A Sunday Afternoon on the Island of La Grand Jatte* (1884) even more because we see it is made up of dots of colour; or when a puppet made out of wood gives the illusion of life. We respond instinctively to visual puns and optical illusions. We enjoy tricks. We know what we are looking at, all the same…

Animation definitely fits in here.

Long ago and far away

A story set long ago can be more critical of current times, and a fantasy land or secret worlds can be more observational of our own world than a more straightforward contemporary setting. The possibilities of talking indirectly about ourselves are endless, and animation itself is one of these possibilities. The artificiality of the medium encourages a lack of inhibition. Who would blame a puppet or a drawn character for behaving outrageously and honestly? Welcome to the world of animation.

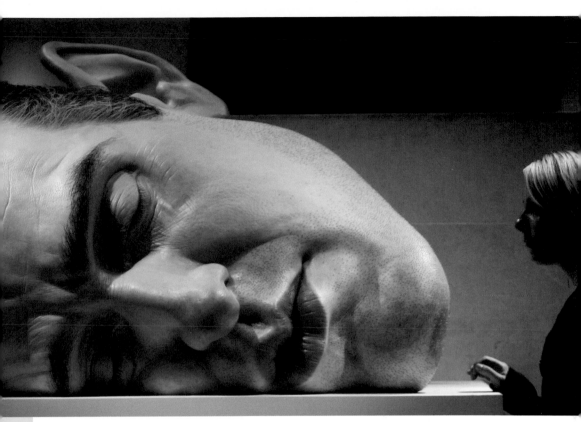

2.3

2.3

Mask II 2001/2002

artist
Ron Mueck
That this artist's sculptures are
so realistic is one thing, but
that they are so unexpectedly
monumental, as with this
room-filling head, is quite
another. Our expectations are
confounded. Cover the lady
viewer with your hand and the
sculpture is just a striking head,
but reveal the viewer again
and the perception of the head
changes dramatically.

At the start of any project there must be a desire to tell a story, to suggest an idea or theme or to show something from a fresh perspective, or merely to comment on something, or make an observation. The way these ideas are conveyed is as important as the story itself, and we have a duty not to be dull. We want people to watch our films after all. However, although the technique of animation is certainly interesting in itself, that alone does not necessarily guarantee sufficiently captivating the audience – you must have something, however small, to say. There must be a journey; a reason to attract the viewers' attention.

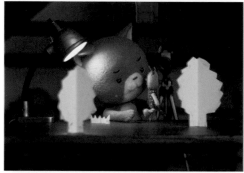

2.4

Komaneko: The Curious Cat
2009

animator
Hirokazu Minegishi
A truly delightful, well-observed series of films from Japan about a stop-motion cat making stop-motion films and the frustrations involved.

2.4

Adding to the technique

There have been great films whose *raison d'être* was to demonstrate the potential of a particular technique, but they are usually great because the narrative uses the technique rather than the technique using the narrative. You really do need a strong idea, and a strong sustained belief in your idea, before approaching stop-motion, if only to justify the sheer effort involved.

You can't begin your story without making a decision about the technique, which will affect absolutely every frame. The technique of stop-motion is unavoidably part of the film, but it shouldn't be what the film is about. It has to be the tool that is the most appropriate way to tell a particular story, and that story must contain elements that could not be realized any other way.

There have been several beautiful stop-motion films about the art of stop-motion itself. These include *The Maker* (2011), *Sleight of Hand* (2012) and *Marionette* (2012), and a delightful Japanese series, *Komaneko*, about a stop-motion cat making stop-motion films, but rather than these being an indulgent excuse to showcase our craft, they are all poignant looks at the relationship between the artist and art, and raise profound questions about the nature of art and life and why we do it, and, actually, by questioning who we are we acknowledge our existence. That must be one of the most fundamental themes of all drama. The gloriously haunting Australian short film *Sleight of Hand* teases the audience with what they are watching, and then along the way flirts with the secrets of stop-motion as the protagonist questions his existence. My own film, *Tchaikovsky – An Elegy* (2011), whilst not directly referencing stop-motion, theatrically shows the character forced to evaluate his existence and his worth. There is a real fascination with how art works today, with hundreds of DVDs and books full of 'the making of...' themes. Exposing the mechanics of theatre and film does not in any way ruin the experience. Rather, it allows us to invest in the illusion, bringing us closer to the shared experience through contributing. Once again, it is about not being ashamed to enjoy the artifice.

The three unities

Although there are tricks, tips, clichés, structures and devices for making stories work, there are no hard and fast rules to writing a story for animation (or for any other medium) these days, and if there were rules, they would be challenged. However, the plays of the ancient Greeks were structured to follow the three unities laid down by Aristotle (384 BC–322 BC). These rules demanded that there be one main plot, one location and that all the action should take place within 24 hours. It was also suggested that the plays should include no more than two characters, and sometimes the chorus, on stage at any one moment. You won't go wrong by keeping it simple, uncluttered and direct – thank you Aristotle. These rules gave the Greek plays an enviable focus and economy, but they were eventually broken. Shakespeare consciously acknowledged the rules and then flouted them. This is trumpeted in the opening of *Henry V*, which directly asks the audience to imagine many shifts of location and time and spectacle that couldn't be presented literally. This wasn't just a creative solution to budgetary constraints and limited resources. It was enjoying the artifice of theatre and, rather than being literal and functional, it was inviting the audience to be part of the storytelling.

Back with the Greeks, it's pertinent that their choruses in the dramas were masked, in effect making them slightly distant and artificial, almost a puppet; enabling the characters of the chorus to become madcap birds, scared citizens, avenging furies, or even abstractions, usually offering contentious or moralistic ideas of how the upright citizens of Athens should live. An early example of artifice being truthful and honest.

The expensive business of animation often necessitates films made with painstaking and constant reference to focus groups and relentless analysis of target audiences, but I'd be sad to see those most basic elements of storytelling, imagination and instinct, consumed by mechanical formulae. There is a box. Think outside of it.

First, have a definite, clear practical ideal; a goal, an objective. Second, have the necessary means to achieve your ends; wisdom, money, materials and methods. Third, adjust all your means to that end.
Aristotle

2.5

2.5

Harvie Krumpet 2003

director
Adam Elliot
The Krumpets, from Adam Elliot's
moving film *Harvie Krumpet,*
where a complex and tragic story
is beautifully contrasted with the
deliberately simple animation.

Exercise: Shop window stories

Have a look at three seemingly unlinked
objects in a shop window and try to make
a story or connection between them. Find a
character the audience will love and establish
relationships between the three objects,
and then find the drama within the setting.
Imagine what happens in their secret world
when the public aren't looking. Is the image of
the objects in the window the end of the story
or actually the start? Can stop-motion make
these stories more interesting?

Shakespeare's theatres were constructed
to involve the audience; letting them use
their imaginations by sharing the 'trick'.
Lady Macbeth holding a candle was all
that was needed to suggest night – and
then there's the convention of female roles
played by men; a convention the audience
happily accepted, if the performance was
strong. The raised stage was not about
separation but about focus. There was
no **proscenium,** and no curtain in front
of the stage, which, certainly for me,
can generate a 'them and us' feeling, as
can a cinema screen. A stage curtain or
proscenium can become a barrier to the
audience connecting with the piece – it
forms a very bold visual division.

Cinema has its own distancing proscenium
in the form of the edges of the frame. We
need to play with space and depth and
focus to help the viewer feel that they are
not just looking at the screen but entering
into the action. After Shakespeare, many
theatre stages retreated behind prosceniums,
offering spectacle behind a frame. Happily,
that trend is reversing and it's becoming more
common for actors to share the same space
as the audience, making the whole event a
shared experience. As animators, our work
is usually seen on one plane (other than 3D
feature films) and our job is to gently coax the
audience into our world. Stop-motion, with its
natural use of spatial dimension, is an easier
world to enter than most animation.

2.6

2.6

Next 1989

director
Barry JC Purves
Audiences were encouraged
to use their imaginations in
Shakespeare's productions;
they were aware of the artifice
of theatre but still became
involved in the action. This film
is an acknowledgement of many
of Shakespeare's conventions
with an animated twist,
whilst celebrating the joy of a
puppet performing.

Automata

To some extent stop-motion animators are the natural descendants of all the artisans and craftsmen working with clockwork who for centuries strove to give automata and figures in dazzling medieval clock towers an independent, convincingly realistic life – often a life that prompted much philosophical debate about the very nature of life. The animator's hand working invisibly between frames has made the clockwork redundant, but whilst automata perform live many times, our once-only performance exists merely in the cold distance of film.

Some of these exquisite automata needed just a key to coax intricate cogs and cams into giving the character an illusion of life; others, ironically, as in the case of a legendary chess-playing automata, needed a human discreetly hidden away. We are happy, these days, to see the mechanics of such tricks – seeing the operators of the astonishing puppets from Handspring Puppet Company in the National Theatre's iconic *War Horse*, only increases the pleasure of the illusion. We can't get away from the fact that puppets, in whatever form, need a puppeteer, and that relationship really is part of the joy.

The uncanny valley

This has become a rather overused, odd and glibly dismissive expression, referring mainly to computer animation, though it could apply to sophisticated stop-motion, where the animation and characters are convincingly realistic but where some spark of life is missing. The viewers are confused as to what they are actually looking at, and don't connect with the character. This was first discussed in relation to humanoid robots and automata – when they became too lifelike, spectators reacted negatively towards them. It's a disconcerting effect – so perfectly real and yet so dead. In animation, this can be combatted through the skills of performance-based animators, who are able to add all the quirks and changes of rhythm and nuance that bring a character to life.

The **proscenium** is the part of the theatre stage in front of the curtain that frames the action and hides the mechanics of how the production works.

The most important 'rule' in any form of storytelling is that you must keep your audience interested in your characters and situations. Anger your audience, challenge them, thrill them, seduce them, but never bore them. This requires the exploitation and thorough understanding of the medium you're using. You can keep the audience interested not just through an enormous range of inventive narrative techniques (such as pacing, revelations, suspense, flashbacks, clues and so forth), but also through the full use of all the sensory elements of film-making – such as design, sound, movement, lighting, costume, camera work, and editing.

However you choose to achieve it, it is vital that you keep the audience wanting to look at the screen, eager to know what happens next to the characters, especially the main protagonist. Stop-motion can be included as one of the elements that intrigue an audience, but it is not a narrative element in itself. What interests an audience is the fate of the characters as well as their goals, the obstacles they have to overcome and the ways they deal with their situation. We need to take an interesting journey, however small, with our characters.

Non-literal representation

Animation often works best when the action and characters are not presented as literal representations of reality. Animation works most triumphantly when it acknowledges its artificiality and plays with its own tricks and limitations. Look how little more than a metal box on caterpillar tracks, in *Wall-E* (2008), is able to suggest strong emotions. Or how simple line drawings evoke recognizable situations and lumps of Plasticine create whole complex characters, or how a simple character clearly made out of fabric can proffer profound thoughts as in *Oh Willy...*. A good way to test if your idea might revel in the artificiality of animation is to ask: Could this story be told better in live action? If the answer is 'yes' then it may be time to think again. If the answer is 'no!' then the process of animation may truly add a new, engaging perspective to your story.

2.7

The Nightmare Before Christmas 1993

director
Henry Selick
This classic film answers a resounding 'no!' when asked if it could have been done better in live action. Every design choice, every proportion and odd movement is so appropriate to animation, especially stop-motion. And with the clash of two worlds, a change of perspective is a great illuminating narrative device.

Focusing the idea

Animated stories

As animators we have the liberty to exploit all the elements of storytelling and design and movement and character, bringing them all together for one unified whole. Such liberty might be wasted on faithful representations of reality, but stories of secret worlds, fantastic creatures, skewed perspectives and stylistic innovation all thrive in animation.

Animation is a form of art and many dazzling films prefer to concentrate on a visual idea or technique, and not a narrative. Indeed, many lauded films are little more than a succession of colours or shapes, some scratched directly onto the film – such as Richard Reeves' brilliant *Linear Dreams* (1998).

But if you are trying to develop a narrative in your film, it would be a shame not to enjoy the tricks of this medium. That does not necessarily mean filling your story with the undead, robots, dinosaurs or talking animals – all of which are favourite subjects of animated films. But it does mean finding a fluid reality or a twisted perspective to your story. It's certainly helpful to have a central active character with whom the viewer can identify, and to whom extraordinary things happen, finding themselves in conflict with an inverted world or who overcomes obstacles. Lewis Carroll's *Alice in Wonderland* is hugely appealing to animators as it incorporates all of these features. Alongside Disney's 1951 version, there is a remarkable 1988 stop-motion feature by Jan Švankmajer, and the recent film by Tim Burton was full of groundbreaking CG special effects. The Royal Ballet has a spectacular version in their repertoire that mixes animation, breathtaking projections, huge puppets and ravishing design and dancing.

Wonderland offers young Alice a view of her life seen from a very new perspective, full of adults behaving very oddly. As in most fantasies, it is grounded in a very solid but twisted logic – it sort of makes sense, after having seen cats without smiles, to see a smile without a cat. It's this lateral thinking that is so right for animation. Superficially, Alice is very much a gentle Sunday afternoon ramble full of pondering life's curiosities, but even so, there is a central character facing elements of the ticking clock; of a final destination; of many obstacles to overcome; of extraordinary changes of perspective and size; of puzzles to be solved, and all driven by the fear of losing one's head! Alice also has a satisfying structure of slipping from one world to another and back again, thanks to the evocative rabbit hole, and most stage and film productions use the wonderland characters as echoes of Alice's real life. Does your story have such a change of perspective and tension? If not, do find your rabbit hole.

2.8

Alice (Něco z Alenky) 1988

director
Jan Švankmajer
Alice and her associated host of eccentric characters are constantly reinvented; the metaphors fuelling artists' different agendas. Sometimes cute, and sometimes deeply disturbing and disturbed, as here with Švankmajer's White Rabbit.

A change of perspective is invariably illuminating, as characters such as Charles Dickens' Scrooge painfully realized. The visiting apparitions, again characters of artifice, showed him quite drastically what life could be if he did not mend his ways. For this reason, a change of perspective is always a fruitful place to start a story. This shift can be dramatized through a conflict between two worlds such as in Tim Burton's *Corpse Bride* (2005) and Laika's *ParaNorman*. In a pleasing twist, the reality of Disney's *Enchanted* (2007) was the animated world, and the live-action world became the fantasy world. The conflict can be between two worlds, or two generations, or two cultures, or two genders – but the protagonists do need to see themselves through each other's eyes. The catalyst for this need not be geographical but could be a strange outsider such as ET, Mary Poppins, Peter Pan or even a red balloon in the classic children's film *The Red Balloon* (1956).

Writers and dramatists use this displacement as a device for eventually seeing oneself or one's world clearly. Most such stories begin by setting up a situation that's comfortable, which is then complicated or changed through threats, quests, visitations, secrets, revelations, ambition, oppositions, deprivations and achievements. These are then resolved after some sort of journey and confrontation. The more obstacles that are overcome by the main character, the richer the conclusion.

In fantasy worlds, the main characters see what is familiar in a new and different light. Films such as *Madame Tutli-Putli* (2007) and *Coraline* (2009), where the reality of the story is somewhat fluid, lend themselves perfectly to stop-motion. *Coraline* particularly has a disturbing world of 'others' – a very twisted variation on the heroine's family. The pure physicality of the puppets and sets add credibility to the fantasy. Drawn and CG animation have no boundaries and anything is possible, but stop-motion is grounded by this physicality and the fantasy is stronger where it overcomes these limitations.

2.9

2.9

ParaNorman 2012

directors
Chris Butler and Sam Fell
The conflict between the living
and the dead are a recurring
theme in animation; a satisfyingly
ironic idea as animators are, in
effect, giving life to the non-living.
Here are Norman and his two,
beautifully designed, families.

Fantasy, fable and allegory

A film about a robot stranded on a planet picking up rubbish is certainly about the problems facing such a robot, but at its core *Wall-E* is much more a story about the human condition, loneliness and the need for a partner. Fish may not conduct father-and-son relationships, but *Finding Nemo* was certainly more about that than observations about marine life. Similarly, *Pinocchio* (1940) is less about the inner workings of a puppet than about the dilemma every one of us has faced: that of facing emotional responsibilities as we grow up.

To some extent, putting well-observed life lessons into the voices of animals, robots or cars can be seen as using 'a spoonful of sugar to help the medicine go down', but it's also about using fantasy, fable and allegory to show the truth directly and selectively.

Often, a visual metaphor is simply stronger and more appealing than the cold hard truth; something Aesop, Hans Christian Andersen and others knew all too well. Imagine how less interesting it would have been had George Orwell not put his politics into the mouths of pigs in *Animal Farm* or if the four Pevensie children hadn't gone through the wardrobe into the land of Narnia but had instead been straightforwardly told the story of Christ. These metaphors also remove much of the clutter associated with more realistic, complex human characters, while also giving storytellers the opportunity to make witty comparisons. Most fables and fairy tales have animals centre stage. In truth, most have little to do with animals but are using the animal to say something selective about the human condition.

2.10

2.10

Life's a Zoo 2008

creators
Adam Shaheen and Andrew Horne II
Morreski, and friend, from *Life's a Zoo*. This series uses vividly realized characters to satirize reality shows and highlight many racial stereotypes.

Focusing the idea

2.11

2.11

Animal Farm 1954

directors
Halas and Batchelor
Halas and Batchelor's glorious
Animal Farm; anthropomorphism
at its most didactic
and digestible.

Exercise: Out of this world

Taking a character from one world
and transporting them to another,
twisted reality is a much-loved trick
of authors and animators. Make
a list of five of your favourites, such
as, *The Wizard of Oz* (1939) or
H. G. Wells' *The First Men in the
Moon* and consider how you might
make the shift between realities
visually or aurally clear. Consider the
sudden jump to glorious Technicolor
when Dorothy arrives in Oz, or
Coraline's 'other' parents' button
eyes, or Alice's changing size in
Wonderland.

How would you achieve the same
effect in your story?

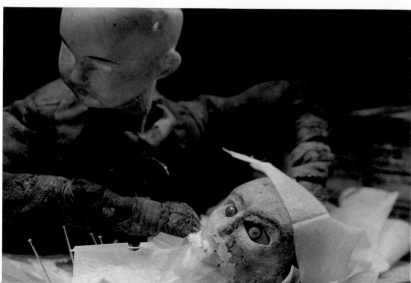

The Brothers Quay

Animators such as the Brothers Quay don't just offer a change of perspective, they make up their own. Their worlds are totally unique and bear scant relation to our world. Their characters often appear to inhabit a secret world made up of things we have discarded, or events that seem to be happening behind our backs. Theirs is a world that is so appropriate to stop-motion, relying on broken objects, often dolls, and textures, with very real materials being imbued with some purpose, and all enjoying the quirky movement of our particular animation technique. Simple everyday objects, such as a comb, can take on a huge significance. This is one of their strengths; they can give even a screw being tightened in a piece of wood some tension and drama and an emotional resonance. Why shouldn't such objects have their own stories and meanings and nightmares? Have a look at the objects around you, and ponder how they got there. What is their backstory?

2.12
___

Street of Crocodiles 1986

directors
The Brothers Quay
From broken dolls and abandoned objects, the Brothers Quay produce disturbing films unlike any others, full of menace, where even the smallest forgotten article is given unsettling resonances.

Getting away with it

Another reason to tell your story through animation or puppetry is that they can say and do things that a real person cannot. Puppets have a many-centuries-long tradition of verbally attacking institutions or public figures and getting away with it. Who wants to be seen as being outraged by slander from a puppet? Animated TV series such as *Rick and Steve – The Happiest Gay Couple in All the World* (2007–2009), *Life's a Zoo*, *Spitting Image* (1984–1996), *The Simpsons* (1989–), *South Park* (1997–), and *Headcases* (2008), as well as the gloriously outrageous *Team America: World Police* (2004), have indulged in joyously offensive behaviour that live actors might not carry off, or which might have repercussions for the actors themselves. However, outlandish behaviour is nothing without an element of recognizable truth. By hiding behind animated puppets the animator can be more liberated and, ultimately, more honest and observant. Look at Jiří Trnka's poetic but potent *The Hand* (1965) and Jan Švankmajer's *Death of Stalinism in Bohemia* (1991) to see examples of powerful political metaphor.

So, if you have found yourself a story about human relations or concerns, would it be liberated and illuminated by being told using animals or ants or robots? Is it too controversial to have human characters acting it out? Have you found an angle, a perspective, a distancing device, that will allow your story to be truthful?

There has to be a reason for using animation, other than the undeniable but indulgent joy of being directly responsible for bringing things to life or creating strange and exotic environments. Animation has to add something to your film that live action and a few special effects cannot; and that 'something different' usually involves a shift of perspective, metaphor, parody and satire.

2.13

Life's a Zoo 2008

animator
Cuppa Coffee Studios
Animals behaving badly! Using puppets, especially as non-human characters, allows storytellers to say and do things that people couldn't get away with. This distancing is one of the oldest tools of storytelling – and it is still enormously effective.

2.13

A short scene from Disney's *Mary Poppins* (1964) sums up perfectly the point of animation, although ironically this scene is live action. Mary is leaving the family she has healed. She's a bit tearful and agrees politely with her talking parrot umbrella that perhaps the family could have been more grateful. The parrot is about to launch into an honest tirade against the family, but Mary quietly clamps its mouth shut – she doesn't really need to hear a truth that she knows already but can't voice. Surely the point of animation is to say things, or to point out ideas, that can't be expressed in our everyday lives? Here, a puppet, a talking umbrella, is used to project Mary's real feelings. Projection is certainly a word loved by therapists.

Ventriloquists, often with puppets that visually echo their operators, are certainly more liberated and outspoken than their partners. Only rarely do you encounter introverted dummies. This really is about alter egos running riot. We should also mention the liberating effect that puppets have with children who are less able to speak freely. A tactile puppet as a non-judgemental third party can offer such comfort, and release so much – as my teddy, who sits next to me, can testify.

Ciphers

As we've already seen, Shakespeare is full of distancing devices that allow the situation and emotions to be revealed succinctly. One of the most notable uses of artifice is the play within a play in *Hamlet*. Hamlet stages a play containing a heightened version of a murder of a king that echoes the murder of Hamlet's own father, which is so integral to the plot. Whilst Hamlet is unable to accuse him directly, Claudius' reactions to the play expose his guilt. Once again, something full of artifice provokes honesty. I'm tempted to talk about getting away with murder, but that's not quite relevant to Hamlet. However, many a horror film plot has seen a murder committed through a puppet, leaving the puppeteer seemingly innocent.

So often, like Mary Poppins' parrot, drama needs this kind of device or character, and often a most private one, which lets the main character externalize their thoughts. In animation, Jiminy Cricket in *Pinocchio* is a prime example and, at the other extreme, in the gloriously irreverent film, *Marquis* (1989), the live actors have animal masks, and the Marquis de Sade, imprisoned in the Bastille, has an animatronic talking penis that acts as his conscience. Similarly, the great play, *Harvey*, gives the main character not only tongue-loosening alcohol but also an invisible six-foot tall rabbit to talk to. A suggestion of mental unbalance here allows an extra degree of speaking the unspoken. Similarly, the superhero persona is usually more honest than the repressed civilian, just as Mr Hyde was the true character behind Dr Jekyll. To this incomplete list we can add cross-dressing, the simple red noses of clowns,

Focusing the idea

2.14

Homer Simpson's yellow skin, the big comedy shoes of silent comedians, uniforms – there are so many distancing devices that allow us to show the real us. It's ironic that the word 'mask' implies something hidden, when in effect it reveals so much. There are so many ways to change the perspective to see the truth.

2.14

Mary Poppins 1964

director
Robert Stevenson
Mary Poppins and her perceptive umbrella, saying all the things she can't express herself. The visiting mysterious outsider, who causes a family to see themselves afresh, is a great narrative device, and can be seen in classics such as the *Nutcracker*, *Peter Pan* and *ET*.

2.15

2.15

Balance 1989

directors
**Christoph and
Wolfgang Lauenstein**
A film that finds a succinct visual
metaphor for a very human
dilemma. Here, characters find
themselves on a suspended slab
and their existence depends on
cooperation and trust. Animation
is particularly suitable for
these metaphors.

2.16

Speaking honestly

Has the main character in your film got an interesting way of revealing his inner thoughts quite naturally, rather than just saying what he feels? Try to structure your story so that this device allows the characters to see their dilemmas clearly, or to speak their thoughts honestly. This can be anything from a change of technique, or narrative convention, to an imaginary companion. Also, for us as storytellers, it's so much easier to talk honestly through a third person, or from behind a mask, or through a metaphor, and animation (particularly puppets) fulfils this role beautifully.

The beautiful film *The Quest* (1996) is a great example, with its simple character emerging out of the dry sand with a single desire. He is tormented by the sound of dripping water, and his quest is simply to quench his thirst. This quest takes him through several richly textured landscapes, before falling into the water, and once more returning to lifeless sand, and the cycle begins again. The human experience in a mere ten minutes.

2.16

Nina Conti and Monkey

Ventriloquist Nina Conti was given a 'vent' puppet on the death of her partner, Ken Campbell, which was sculpted to resemble him. Her interaction with the puppet acted as catharsis and she was able to talk through it of her grief. She also has an astonishingly honest double act with her current puppet, Monkey.

Recommended viewing

Balance (1989) is a fantastic example of the strength of metaphor. It records the plight of five characters existing on a floating slab in the middle of a void. They all move in synch with each other in order to keep the platform balanced. However, this harmony is disrupted when one character drags a box onto the platform, which everyone wants to investigate. Greed is probably the motivation here, and the ruin of the others. The resultant movements unbalance the platform and all but one character is either pushed or falls into space. The final character is left precariously balanced with the box out of reach.

We don't need to know who the characters are, nor how they got there – let alone how the great slab is suspended – but the image is a great metaphor for mistrust and cooperation. Some writers might pen several volumes to express the futility and frustration experienced in a few minutes by these characters.

Dreams and nightmares

Animation is often described as having a dreamlike or nightmarish quality. This effect can be the result of jumbling up familiar events into surreal contexts, where unconnected concerns and events start to have terrifying or joyous links, and where, literally, anything can happen. In addition to the dreamlike feeling they can produce, dream sequences have been a standby part of even the earliest stop-motion. They allow the narrative to easily showcase animation, special effects and other such tricks.

Dreams are a convention beloved of writers and dramatists because they permit information to be conveyed to the audience, or to reveal a character's inner thoughts, their hopes, or a backstory. This somewhat overused device could be seen as a rather lazy and far too-convenient option. For this reason, dream scenarios work best when the protagonist, or in fact the audience, is unaware of being in a dream or where there is an element of doubt as to what is real and what is not. Many films are based on dreams, but they are usually little more than an excuse for a series of imaginative images. In the real world, even the flimsiest of dreams start with some thought or theme; they illuminate familiar subjects with a new light; dreams, through wild artifice, often bring some coherence to our concerns. They are that change of perspective.

A dream narrative, then, works best when given some logic, however twisted, and some perspective that reflects on the reality, rather than being the justification for some striking but unconnected visuals. There is little more disappointing than being told in the final frames that… 'it was all a dream'.

2.17

2.17

Slumberless 2013

director and animator
Simon Partington
The simple haunted face of
the character from *Slumberless*.
No dreams for him.

Exercise: Dreams

Have a look at how dreams have been used
in films, plays and literature, and see if you
feel the dream device is too convenient, or
whether some element of the character or
plot has been illuminated. Try to remember
one of your own dreams and structure it
into a short scenario that says something
about your own experience or emotions of
that day, making the most of the change of
perspective. Is the dream saying something
you can't? Is it making sense of your fears
and hopes?

Not just for kids

The idea of cartoons or puppets tackling serious and mature themes or documentary subjects can initially seem odd, as we are conditioned to thinking of animation as something for children. However, most subjects and nearly all genres have been tackled in animation.

Sometimes the self-conscious tricks of animating get in the way without connecting to the subject. On other occasions the animation can be seen to trivialize an important subject. However, one of the strengths of animation, its allegorical nature, is to let us see things free of stereotype, free of clutter and free of blinkers.

The film *Zero* (2010) follows a character made of string, marked with a zero. He is alone and the zero implies some worthlessness. In a gorgeously witty and moving final visual pun, his world has significance and worth. Not many writers can express that notion so directly. A picture is indeed worth a thousand words. An animated one even more!

Similarly, there have been at least three animated versions of *The Diary of Anne Frank*, all technically excellent, and sensitive, but with the story based on such real and vivid tragedy, they have been uncomfortable experiences. This may be because the literal approaches to the animation seem inadequate to convey such complex emotions. It is hard to even begin to conceive a puppet version of Anne Frank, although we should avoid the idea that there are some subjects that we have to shy away from. But if you are going to tackle a topic as sensitive as this then be sure you are using the most appropriate approach. Such serious themes often work best when treated through metaphor and heavy styling. But there is no doubting that, when handled well, animation can move an audience to tears – we only need remember those traumatic moments of a mother's death in *Bambi* (1942), and the mother's madness in *Dumbo* (1941), and tears are not far away. More recently, the closing moments of Adam Elliot's *Mary and Max* had audiences, particularly this audience, weeping.

A puppet, being related to sculptures, effigies, icons, statues, dolls, tombs and such, where human contact has given it narrative and emotive resonances, is an object with the potential of allegory built in. When working with puppets we have a metaphor in our hands; myths, as it were, in our mitts. Stop-motion can use this to its advantage.

2.18

Zero 2010

writer, director and animator
Christopher Kezelos
producer
Christine Kezelos
The lonely, lovely ball of string characters in *Zero*.

2.18

When developing your story, do consider the logistics it will require. The economics of stop-motion and of physically building puppets mean that it is rarely practical to structure a script around dozens of characters that only appear briefly on screen. Once you have gone to all the trouble of building a puppet you might as well make the most of it. He or she exists and that's one of the major expenses covered. If you have a puppet it makes little difference, other than general wear and tear to the puppet, whether the character has to carry a short film or a feature. This is in stark contrast to a drawn film or a clay film where the character has to be redrawn and re-sculpted for every scene.

So much effort and expense goes into the making of puppets that it's best to concentrate on fewer characters. This, of course, tightens a narrative and you need to be ingenious in finding ways to suggest incidental characters or crowds. The *Wallace and Gromit* half-hour specials have few secondary characters, but with clever storytelling and strong relationships the world of West Wallaby Street doesn't look underpopulated.

The budget for my own short, *Tchaikovsky – An Elegy* only permitted the building of one puppet, and needed extreme invention to find ways of referring to characters in Tchaikovsky's life without building them as puppets. As usually happens, such economics usually work to the film's advantage. Do not close your mind to keeping the number of characters and set to a minimum. The big stop-motion films of 2012, *ParaNorman*, *The Pirates! In an Adventure with Scientists* and *Frankenweenie* were certainly peopled with dozens of characters but happily had budgets that could support them.

2.19

Toby's Travelling Circus
2012–

director
Barry JC Purves
In the TV series *Toby's Travelling Circus*, our necessary audience in the Big Top are no more than heads on rough bodies, and judiciously placed graphic cut-outs. An occasional head turn, a rather rigid waving arm and suitable sound effects keep them alive.

Focusing the idea

2.19

Crowds

For CG films there are a range of programs to replicate characters into vast crowds, each slightly different in look and behaviour. It is, of course, different in stop-motion where featuring dozens of different characters, apart from being dramatically suspect, would be impractical.

That said, however, crowd scenes are not impossible in stop-motion. There are various optical and staging tricks to help, but if you're shooting a crowd scene you are going to get only a few seconds of animation shot in a day. I shot a commercial involving 32 Viennese Whirls, dressed in sashes and gloves, dancing to Strauss' *Emperor Waltz* in a ballroom. Thanks to a well-placed mirror and some devious choreography, we managed to raise that number considerably – a trick used early in Starewicz's films. Of course, computer graphics and green screens help today, and shooting on digital does allow you to reproduce characters into a crowd.

Making a little go a long way

A stop-motion film full of characters walking and running is going to be much more complex and time-consuming to shoot than a film full of talking heads. So when you're planning your film do think about what you really need to show on screen and what you can simply imply. *Gargoyle* (2005) by Michael Cusack, manages to tell a haunting story with just two characters. It is satisfying to spend so much time with such well-crafted characters. His most recent film, *Sleight of Hand*, again has just two figures.

My own films have concentrated on minimal characters and with *Tchaikovsky – An Elegy*, I had but one. Any necessary crowd puppets and secondary characters, and I do always question if they are necessary, have been less sophisticated puppets. Whilst developing *Plume*, it was always intended that there be four shadowy characters. The budget allowed three, which turned out for the best, as three characters provided better choreography when attacking the main character – one on each arm and one on the back. Having four would have left one spare.

Another tactic is to give your 'extras' interchangeable elements to make them go further. The courtiers in an early scene in *Rigoletto* (1993) appeared a short while later redressed and dirtied up as beggars. Such is life!

The level of expression required from your character and how accurate the lip synch needs to be both add to the expense of your puppet. If you are happy with limited movement in the faces, it will save considerably on the budget but will put more focus on the body language, and the need to have a sophisticated armature. This in turn affects the storytelling.

It is essential to have a clear idea of just how the narrative will work before designing the characters. If the film is told mainly in wide shots, costly facial mechanics or more squash-and-stretchy replacement pieces would be redundant. Not so if there are many close-ups. Maybe you need a general wide-shot puppet, and a more detailed close-up puppet. If the character is confined to a chair or is only seen in bed, does it really need articulated legs? If you're thinking that at some point it might walk then make sure you make that decision during the storyboard stage of pre-production. Hands, by their very nature, are complicated to make, so ask yourself just how expressive they need to be. It's an odd way to budget films, but certain activities, gestures and expressions are more expensive than others, and this must be taken into account. The budget and narrative are unlikely bedfellows.

2.20

2.20

The Maker 2011

director
Christopher Kezelos
A touching still from *The Maker*,
where a puppet movingly
creates another to pass on
his experience.

Exercise: Essentials

Take a well-known story, film or
play and see how far you can pare
down the number of characters and
locations, and find devices that might
impart plot and information otherwise
done by minor characters. You can
turn this reduction into something
creative. Again, it is all about not
being literal. Most animation is about
telling the biggest stories with only the
most essential elements.

Keep out of the water

Animation can certainly do most things, but you'd be giving yourself unnecessary headaches by making a film where most of the stop-motion characters spend their time indulging in such activities as swimming or flying. The sheer practicalities of supporting characters for such actions, while a rewarding challenge, must lead a producer to consider other techniques. The need for so much water in the plot prompted Aardman's *Flushed Away* (2006) to be achieved through CG animation, as was the sea in their recent *The Pirates! In an Adventure with Scientists!*. The watery *Finding Nemo* would have been extraordinarily difficult with stop-motion – especially the translucent jellyfish. On the other hand, a film like *Cars* (2006) might have worked well in stop-motion, depending on how flexible the cars needed to be, though the essence of speed would have been hard to capture without blurring.

The point is that you must consider the technical and practical aspects of your characters when approaching a story. Fluffy, floaty, smoky, hairy, wispy, floppy, stretchy, sticky, transparent, wet – all would be cause for grief if treated through stop-motion. None of them is impossible, but puppets have an undeniable physical presence that is best exploited. This is their strength; make use of it.

2.21

2.21

There There 2003

director
Chris Hopewell
This music video for Radiohead's song *There There*, by Chris Hopewell of Collision Films, not only features large numbers of stop-motion characters, but is mixed with live action and shot on a tight budget. Quite a feat.

Focusing the idea

2.22

Plume 2011

director
Barry JC Purves
My film *Plume* had both
swimming and flying, but that
was part of the challenge and the
water sequence was beautifully
handled by Dark Prince, the
production company, as CG.
This has caused some questions
about changing from stop-
motion to CG midway through
a film, but in the context of the
story it was necessary for the
character, who found himself in
an environment that was both
the same and different from what
he had known before.

2.23

Fur and feathers!

Animation and animals go hand in hand, or paw in paw, and with animals and birds come fur and feathers – a lot of them. But if you are using stop-motion for a story with furry characters then be prepared for a certain amount of crawling (movement and twitching in the fur caused by the animator's constant touching of the puppets), although that didn't take anything away from King Kong in 1933. The alternative is to spend a huge amount of expensive, inventive work in the manufacture of the puppets to avoid the crawling. The puppets in *Fantastic Mr. Fox* do have fur, but they were designed to reduce crawling to a minimum, and thanks to the heavy styling of the film, some crawling became part of the home-made charm, reminding the audience of the presence of the animator.

Often puppets' fur is sculpted as part of the latex or silicon skin, with strands of hair to confuse the issue. Another approach is to make the fur stylized. There is, again, no getting away from the fact that puppets are touched every frame, and with textures such as fur and cloth, this can be a problem. Likewise, long hair drawn onto a character in the design stage looks beautiful, but the practicalities are another matter. If not animated, it looks unnatural and lifeless. If animated, an awful amount of time will be consumed. The flopping strands of hair on the *Frankenweenie* puppets were the result of an extraordinary amount of complex mechanical ingenuity and brilliant animation. Can you create an equally interesting design look but without the long hair? As always, it is a balance between the creative and the practical.

It is important to think carefully about exactly what will be required of the puppets. The furry characters in *Monsters Inc.* (2001), especially Sully, would have been impossible in stop-motion, and I suspect this is a challenge that excited the CG animators for that reason; and a challenge that was celebrated in the long luxurious red hair in Pixar's *Brave* (2012) and the tiger's fur in *The Life of Pi* (2012). CG does fur so much better, and to attempt a detailed fur in clay and drawings would be foolhardy. *Pi*'s Richard Parker is an overwhelming CG creation, an astonishing achievement, indistinguishable from a real tiger.

Essentially, the practicalities and economics cannot be separated from the storytelling, most especially with stop-motion where everything has to be built, and there's less chance of reusing material.

2.23

Pipkin 2013

director
Pamela Wyn Shannon
producer
Linda McCarthy
The beautiful, tactile textures of the characters from *Pipkin* revel in the use of woolly fabrics, which had to be carefully handled to avoid 'crawling'.

Intimacy versus panoramic views

Stop-motion, with its tabletop sets, is able to suggest intimate locations convincingly through the use of close-ups and mid shots. However, restricted budgets, and physical studio space, can often prevent the use of huge wide panoramas and vistas, as these, traditionally, have to be built and take up considerable, expensive space. Sometimes, such as in *Hamilton Mattress* (2002), good old theatrical tricks of false perspective create the illusion of space and scale, but now most stop-motion sets are supplemented through CG and green-screen work, allowing for more scale. Certainly my last two series have seen panoramic shots created in CG.

There's a satisfaction to building as much as possible, and the sets on *ParaNorman*, *Pirates!* and *Frankenweenie* were massive, but even so CG can go further. As you approach your story, do consider the practicalities of where and how it might be filmed. Several of my films have been filmed in small studios (well, small rooms, really), and a stylish fluid black void has been a creative answer to not having the space or budget to build huge sets. This should be considered as early as possible in the production process.

There's no doubt that animators, like actors, prefer working in real, spatial sets, rather than CG environments. However good our imaginations are, we like having tangible props and puppets to interact with.

Who and where?

So, at the end of Chapter 1, we found our drama – but who are the two characters? Here are some key questions to ask yourself as you develop your protagonists:

● Is one character preventing the other from reaching their goal?

● Is the second character a catalyst for the main character's revelations about him- or herself?

● Is it a metaphor or fable, with animals, or robots, or flowers as the main actors? Does that better illuminate their characters?

● Is one of the characters an object that represents the dilemma?

● Do you need dialogue or can you tell the story through movement alone? How do the characters communicate amongst themselves?

● Is the character's journey absolutely clear?

● Where is the action happening? Do you need to be specific or is it a fluid space?

● If there are gags, do they reveal something about the characters or the theme?

As you ponder the characters and settings, think whether you have the resources to realize them. What technique will be best for the characters and for the tone of the film – are they puppets? Clay? Drawn in sand? Discarded objects?

In the next chapter we'll start storyboarding...

3.1

In Chapter 3, we'll find out what qualities a puppet, and objects, can bring to a film that actors, drawn and computer-generated images cannot. We'll look at why stop-motion puppets have an extra element of life and spontaneity about them. We'll also look at how to get the most out of a puppet in design terms. In particular, we'll focus on exploiting the features of a puppet, such as the eyes and the hands, that are best for expression, and how to make them as 'animatable' as possible.

Finally, we will also discuss other techniques that involve physically touching and manipulating objects in front of or under a camera to tell a story. These techniques clearly demonstrate that a complicated puppet is not always necessary to tell an affecting story.

3.1

Tchaikovsky – An Elegy 2011

director
Barry JC Purves
The brilliantly emotive puppet from *Tchaikovsky* was made by Mackinnon & Saunders. Mackinnon & Saunders are UK-based stop-motion puppet makers, sculptors and artists, whose puppets for *Frankenweenie*, *Corpse Bride* and *Fantastic Mr. Fox* have

Puppets, in all their many forms, will never reproduce the complex and multifaceted, idiosyncratic and random movement of live action and that really is not their purpose. They have neither the fluidity of CG nor the freedom of drawn animation – nor should they. As we've seen, they have their own distinct qualities; they exist, and their performance is intrinsically tied up with how they are operated. They have credibility, a tangible presence and a physical distinctiveness of which even the most casual viewer is aware. This is a particular motivation for telling an animated story with puppets and objects.

The fact that big emotions, drama, tension and humour can all be conveyed through what are clearly pieces of brass, wood, fabric, silicon and clay is part of the appeal of puppets and stop-motion. They are credible because they exist as part of a physical world. The effect is not realistic, but the physicality of the puppets gives their actions total plausibility, and an immediate connection with the audience. That they exist in a real space, reacting spontaneously to lights, focus, gravity and to each other, gives the puppets many resonances.

Simple puppets

Complex puppets are not essential for telling a story, and many animators enjoy getting storytelling out of intentionally simple materials. Sometimes animators don't use puppets at all, but use objects or materials such as sand and salt, and when that works the results can be sublime. Creating beautiful, evocative imagery and movement out of something as simple as sand requires inventive technique and a detailed understanding of light, movement, shade and texture. It also requires an equally imaginative approach to storytelling. Getting so much out of so little is enormously gratifying.

The availability of apps on phones and tablets has made it possible to produce an animated film quickly, with whatever is to hand. If it's not great, it can simply be deleted. These films and clips may not get seen beyond Facebook and YouTube, but they are satisfying, and provide the immense pleasure of making something come alive. Probably, when every foot of actual film, subsequent processing, and technical equipment had to be accounted for, the approach was more considered, planned and meticulous. Now it is possible to point and shoot by oneself, filming on the run rather than suffering months of planning. The results may be disposable, but they are still results. And for such guerrilla film-making, you are unlikely to be building vastly complicated characters.

Working with figurative characters may perhaps seem an advantage, but even so the puppet has to be designed to maximize its potential for expression. Some puppets are so elaborate that their constant movement can become counterproductive, and what

The puppets

is being expressed can easily be lost. These overly complex puppets sometimes resolutely refuse to spring into life, as their 'fidgeting' gets in the way of a performance. Conversely, there are puppets and objects that are little more than a block of wood or a discarded object, but a well-timed movement or attitude can suggest an immediately recognizable action or emotion. The secret is in enjoying the puppet, making everything count, and only having what is necessary. Don't feel your film is any the less by being simple – think about what is the best way to tell your story with the facilities you have. Let the story come first, and then find the right way to tell it.

3.2

Tchaikovsky – An Elegy 2011

director
Barry JC Purves
A montage showing the creation of the Tchaikovsky puppet by Mackinnon & Saunders.

The unavoidable truth about any stop-motion puppet or animated object is that the animator is going to have to touch it for every single frame. This is the most appealing aspect of the process. To maintain the necessary poses a puppet usually requires an interior skeleton, an armature, with a robust durability that can also be easily controlled. Here is an inherent contradiction, as we want total flexibility, but we also need the puppet to support itself.

There are many things to think about when creating a puppet. If it is too big, it could be too heavy, requiring the sets to be larger, taking up too much space in the studio. If it is too small, it may be fiddly, but the most important element to consider is that you have to hold it to manipulate it, and you must think of how and where the puppet will be held.

Any stop-motion animation is going to need both hands – animators who casually work with one hand in their pocket astonish me. With your left hand stabilizing and gripping the puppet tightly, usually with an elbow resting on the set for extra solidity, the right hand, acting with leverage, moves only the elements necessary for that frame. Every puppet needs a solid place to grip firmly for this leverage, and in figurative puppets this usually ends up being in the chest area. A block of balsa or a solid framework in the chest is ideal. Using something softer would compress as you gripped the puppet, and may not spring back to the right place, causing unwelcome twitching. Likewise, any fancy piece of costume, such as frills, placed where you will hold the puppet can only get in the way.

The puppet has to be well-constructed and durable, otherwise it simply won't deliver. Think, as you design it, how you are going to hold the puppet.

It's also worth bearing in mind that puppets don't have the physical limitations of actors, and can therefore easily appear to have unlimited stamina. For this reason, it can be effective to give them a believable physical life by creating the illusion of effort and fatigue. To see a puppet take a breath or an unexpected sneeze gives it credibility. Random details add so much to a performance.

3.3

All My Relations 1990

Animator
Joanna Priestley
This image was created with dog food, among other materials, and demonstrates that expensive, complicated puppets aren't always necessary.

3.4

3.4

The Pirates! In an Adventure with Scientists! 2012

directors
Peter Lord and Jeff Newitt
The Pirate Captain has his hand minutely adjusted as he dashes up the stairs (firmly suspended by his head).

There's just something visceral about moving a puppet frame by frame.... There's a magical quality about it. Maybe you can get smoother animation with computers, but there's a dimension and emotional quality to this kind of animation that fits these characters and this story [*Corpse Bride*].
Tim Burton

Armatures

The material used to construct the skeletons and armatures within the puppet will depend largely on the budget you have available. A cheap option is to make a skeleton from simple aluminium wire. These have very limited durability as, once bent, they simply cannot be straightened again. Also, as you bend the wire into a desired shape it may bend elsewhere – causing all sorts of problems with continuity. This can be controlled to some extent by wrapping balsa around the parts you don't want to move. Using aluminium wire (which can be bent easily and has little spring back) will also help. Wire is still far from ideal, though may work for background puppets where limited and less subtle movement will suffice, but for main characters armatures are pretty essential. It's an expense that will be well worth it.

Even a basic armature will help you produce controlled animation. Generally, armatures are a series of ball-and-socket joints linked by rods, which allow flexibility while also giving clean and maintained definition to the limbs. An armature should be capable of fluid, focused and subtle movement, yet should also be rock steady, not drooping when the animator moves away. This contradiction makes it clear that building an armatured skeleton is a complex art, and that the tensioning of a puppet can make or break the animation. It is therefore very important to work closely with the puppet makers and get experience dealing with different kinds of armature. The important factor in all this is that you can control the puppet.

The number of joints, and therefore to some extent the expense of the armature, depends on exactly what you want from your puppet. There's little point in building a multi-jointed spine if all the character does is lay in bed. Go through your script and see exactly what is required of your puppet, and if you can afford an armature, then go for it. One decent puppet is certainly better than several wobbly ones. Once again, structure your film around what you know is achievable with your resources and budget.

3.5

3.5

An armature kit

There are now numerous very affordable and reliable armatures available to buy online in kit form, which you can customize to your needs. Here, we see a very practical and economical armature kit from Animation Toolkit.

Below

Unlike a drawn or a CG character, if a stop-motion puppet lifts a foot it will fall over, and when you are animating it, it will slide around. For this reason, every puppet has to be firmly anchored to the set. Various techniques can help here. Lightweight puppets can be pinned through the feet to a soft board, although this will affect the design of the sets.

Another technique is to have metal plates on the feet and a perforated steel set, under which strong magnets are located and moved about as appropriate. These magnets aren't cheap, and can damage nearby computers or your hands as they snap together, but they are strong and they last; they can allow a puppet to stand on one foot, as long as the joints are suitably tensioned. However, the need for perforated steel will clearly dictate the design of the set and this may not work for the look of your film. These perforations in the steel are essential, not only for focusing the magnetism, but they also allow you to poke pins through for guidance. Using magnets, though, is a speedy way of animating.

However, magnets may be difficult if your character has small feet or delicate paws. An alternative technique is to secure the feet with tie-downs; these are lockable devices that screw through the set into the foot. They have the advantage of gripping the foot tightly, giving a strong impression of the puppet connecting to its environment. It is a slow and fiddly process and requires access under the set for the animator, as well as a great deal of planning and pre-drilling of holes in the set. It's also easy to dislodge the puppet while you are securing it.

3.6

3.6

Screen Play 1992

director
Barry JC Purves
Because of limited access under the set, the feet of the puppets in *Screen Play* contained small magnets to secure them. This was not ideal as it is hard to lift a magnetized foot off the ground. Removable magnets under the set are more practical.
Photograph by Mark Stewart.

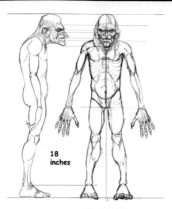

3.7

3.7

Uncle Creepy 2009

directors
Chiodo Brothers
The beginning, middle and end
of the development process
for the Chiodo Brothers' *Uncle
Creepy* puppet.

Outside

Clothes over a puppet remove the need
for detailed sculpting of a body as long as
they are well tailored around basic shapes
attached to the skeleton. These solid shapes,
usually balsa or resin, help keep the silhouette
of the character even after much animation.

With costumed puppets, there's not much
skin on display. If you need to have a naked
or partially naked character then remember
that exposed flesh will get dirty and then need
to be replaced, which can be very expensive.
The all over 'skin' will also make the puppet
considerably heavier, as well as making the
seam lines from the moulding process more
difficult to hide.

In *Oh Willy...,* a clothed character attends
his mother's funeral at a naturist group, and
eventually loses his clothes as well. Everything
in the film is made out of fabric, giving an
extraordinary gentle tactility. Willy's face is
utterly simple and yet conveys so much.
I imagine the puppet was light, and as a result
of being animated the nap of the fabric is alive
in every frame, but this becomes a feature of
the film. Even the dead body has the fabric
gently stirring. The acting is understated with
many strong held poses, but the movement
in the fabric keeps the characters alive. Every
frame is lit to make the most of the texture of
the puppets and sets.

3.8

3.8

Oh Willy... 2012

directors
**Emma De Swaef and
Marc James Roels**
Sensitive lighting shows off the
beautiful textures of the sets
and puppets.

Tip: Skin

The skin for your puppet will depend
on the available budget as well as the
requirements of the animation. Latex
can be baked over the armature in
a mould and painted as necessary.
It has a lovely flesh-like quality;
stretching and wrinkling easily.
However, it has a limited life, tending
to dry and become 'crunchy' after a
while – and it gets dirty very easily.

Silicon is another option that has a
more translucent feel, appropriate
to skin. It lasts longer than latex and
is also easier to clean. On the other
hand, it lacks the flexibility of latex
and is much heavier. A combination
of silicon and latex can also be used,
giving the best of each material.
Plasticine faces are a practical and
economic alternative, but what you
save in construction you will spend
in re-sculpting time, and some detail
will be sacrificed. Of course, there
is no definitive way of creating skin.
This being animation, you could use
any material; newspaper print, felt,
ceramics, leather, silk – anything
appropriate to the design scheme.

In stop-motion animation time is a luxury. It is helpful if your characters are designed to reveal their core characteristics visually and immediately. This is particularly true for short films, which need to make the most of every frame; telling the audience as much as possible, as economically as possible. The puppet's appearance can be the audience's first clue to its character and history. To help this process, many designers think in terms of shapes and silhouettes, and what these say about the characters. It may be hard to imbue a very sharp pointy angular character with much warmth, and conversely, a rounded, wobbly character might find it hard to portray evil. Softness and curves are inevitably associated with cute and cuddly, as are big 'saucer eyes'.

So much can be conveyed from the way a character looks, but animators must also think about how the character will move, and how the moving elements of the design can be used expressively. Think how a tail might be used to show a particular emotion, or whether there are shoulders that can be shrugged. The perfect expression comes when design and movement work together. A haughty character will often be tall, looking down on everyone else, and they will probably walk in a clipped, controlled manner. Conversely, a 'goofy' character will be flexible, saggy, almost boneless and uncoordinated. It's easy to dismiss these design elements as lazy stereotyping, but with limited time to tell your story they are an invaluable visual shorthand.

3.9

3.9

True Family Story 2009

animator
Chris Walsh
Here we have a charming example of pushing and exaggerating human proportions to make characters less literal.

The puppets

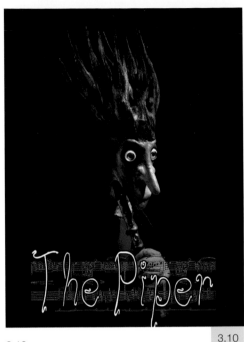

3.10

The Piper 2013

animator
Daniel James
Student Daniel James' startling puppet has a very expressive, easy-to-read face.

3.10

Expressiveness

It's essential when writing and storyboarding your film to think how the characters will express themselves. Will they rely on dialogue, or will they speak to the audience through highly complex facial expressions or lively body language?

Whatever the answer, it will affect the design of the puppet, the storytelling, the rhythm, and camerawork of the film itself. If facial expressions and dialogue are important, you will want to use close-ups, requiring that your puppet can stand the scrutiny of a close-up, where every detail is revealed. The eyes must be alive enough, and focused so that the viewer can read them.

Conversely, if you don't want to tell your story through facial expressions, then a reliance on body language will suggest plenty of wide shots, giving a very different feel to the film. Remember that wide shots take longer to film as there's considerably more to animate. All this, of course, affects the budget. When designing a puppet you need to make sure it is equipped to express what you want the way you want it. Does your puppet have a decent enough skeleton to use its body to act out emotions? Does it have long enough legs to provide those elegant strides you want? Students often draw beautiful storyboards with the characters going through all manner of physical contortions. In reality, this is often impractical for a physical puppet.

3.11

Hinterland 2010

director
Linda McCarthy

The flat ceramic heads of these puppets force the acting to come from body language rather than facial expressions. The flatness of the heads makes a dramatic impact when turned.

3.11

Spatial awareness

An economic design will only work if you make the most of its movement. If your cast consists of a family of eggs, or billiard balls, or footballs, you're going to fight to make any movement and design interesting. The shapes made by billiard balls moving through space will not register unless there is sufficient detail, such as a face, on the ball. It is important to enjoy the movement of your characters, and necessary to find interesting shapes that read from different angles and change as a character moves. An egg spinning won't work until it is given arms, or fluctuations of colour, and then the slightest move will register. It's always worth imagining your characters in silhouette and whether they still read.

Anatomy

The way in which the characters move in a spatial setting is crucial to any stop-motion film. If you give your potentially elegant character short legs, it will dictate a rather comedic walk. If you give your character huge legs, a stride will take him across the set in a few frames, quicker than the other characters. Big fat chunky feet will necessitate lifting the knees higher than usual to allow for the feet to be flicked through. This may be just the effect you're looking for, but remember that every small detail on the puppet will have some bearing on its movement.

If your character is a dog, but you have made it walk on two legs, this will affect the arrangement of the features and how they animate. Sometimes the anatomy of snouts and beaks prevents the audience from seeing both eyes at the same time, except from the front. This will dictate how the head moves, or necessitate a very flexible neck, or a certain attitude with the head. Mouths that are not usually used for talking may have to be moved around a face just to be seen. Look all around you and see just how people's anatomy affects how they move and react. We do need to see the character's eyes for anything to be communicated.

With drawn animation, CG and clay the animators can cheat and give the characters a rather fluid anatomy. Puppets are more solid, having to obey their rigid mechanics. This should not be seen as a drawback but as part of the charm and challenge. Make sure that when you are designing a puppet, all the features work in practical terms. Will the camera see everything, and will the anatomy hinder the animation?

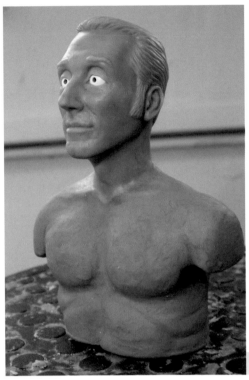

3.12

3.12

Friendly Fire 2008

director
Andreas Kaiser
This soldier in *Friendly Fire*, like most puppets, began its three-dimensional life as a clay model. These can be sculpted until the features are perfected, at which stage a latex or silicon mould is taken.

While a puppet can be subtle it will never have the complex details of live action or CG, but that's not what puppets are about. Puppets are about selective representation. A human face has a multitude of muscles all working together to be expressive, letting the skin stretch, wrinkle and contort. Even the best puppet makers could not duplicate those mechanics and their combinations, and that may not be a bad thing. Puppets work by emphasizing those elements that define the character, and discarding those that have no storytelling value.

In the short *Friendly Fire*, set in the trenches of the First World War, the main characters alternate between live action and animated versions from scene to scene, giving a very fluid and disturbing feel. The film also uses projections of live-action faces onto the puppets, and, conversely, graphics on the live-action faces help blur the line between the two techniques. This blurring perfectly echoes the nightmarish quality of the scenario. It is a remarkable effect, perfect for the film. (However, the mind boggles at the precision of lining up a projector onto the face of a small, moving puppet.) The effect could have been achieved through CG, but it may have been too precise, losing the visceral human element.

On occasion a puppet is too small, which limits the possibility of facial mechanics. A larger, more expressive head can be built for close-ups, but then this does usually require extra bits of set to match, or the use of blue screen. The 1933 King Kong had a full-scale life-size head for certain live-action close-ups and, as it turns out, these were less expressive than the animated puppet.

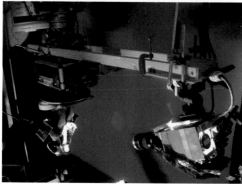

3.13

3.13

Friendly Fire 2008

director
Andreas Kaiser
Here, a puppet has a human actor's face projected onto it. This effect required a complex rig to project the footage accurately and ensure the puppet was very firmly held in place.

The puppets

Being expressive

Live actors can pull as many weird and wonderful facial expressions as they like, and they do, all without adding to the cost of the production. The same cannot be said of stop-motion; it's a peculiarity of this medium that expressions add to the budget, simply because they take longer to create and animate. Therefore, if expressions are an important part of your story, you must think carefully about how these will be achieved.

If your film relies on very complex, detailed expressions CG may be a better solution, but this does depend on how literal you want to be, or how internal or external you want the performance. Several well-known stop-motion television series have recently been turned into CG series, supposedly because CG can provide more facial expressions. This is true, but a good animator can get a huge amount of expression, feeling and character out of a relatively blank face (especially when it is used in conjunction with effective body language). The lack of complicated facial expression is rarely a hindrance to good acting, especially if the puppet has a versatile body and emotive eyes.

An interesting merger of CG and stop-motion, seen in several recent TV series, uses featureless puppets on set. The facial expressions are added through CG afterwards. This technique is also used in the live-action puppet series *Strange Hill High* (2013). This is useful if you are hoping to adapt the same piece of footage for different scenes, but animators would prefer to have the complete performance in their hands. However, there are some situations where expressions on the physical puppet are paramount. In *Rigoletto*, it would have been absurd not to have used expressive faces because the story demanded a great deal of dynamic singing. Bear in mind, though, that focusing on the faces hinders much movement with the body, as an animation camera cannot always follow head movements as a live-action camera can. To go in for close-ups you must make sure that the dialogue and emotion are an essential part of that scene.

Sometimes, facial expressions and body language have such clarity that dialogue becomes redundant. Stop-motion is particularly good at exploiting this idea.

Recommended viewing

Look at the controlled but expressive, rhythmic physicality of Buster Keaton, Max Linder, Jacques Tati and the other silent comedians, to see just how much can be expressed through a static face but a mobile body. Watch the final scene of Keaton's *One Week* (1920) to see emotions from desperation to disappointment to love – all expressed without a word.

Stop-motion puppets needing expressive faces usually rely on an internal skull with a complex arrangement of levers and paddles attached to an outer skin. This can produce a huge variety of expressions, with the advantage that you can spontaneously decide whether to have a large increment one frame and a small one the next. Obviously, such mechanics are expensive (unless you have the skills to make them yourself), and add to the weight of the puppet, which can sometimes make the puppets top heavy, or lead to necessarily large heads to cope with the mechanics inside. Some of the levers can be manipulated by fingers or shaped lollipop sticks – others need keys and special tools. Elements where the movement could fight the natural tension of the artificial skin, such as a widely opening jaw, might need a geared device to hold it open.

A way to get round the need for interior mechanics is to use replacements – literally replacing a fixed face, or elements of a face, such as a mouth, with a completely new piece, and thus suggesting a move. This does, however, require a great deal of planning during the storyboard stage so you know in advance exactly how many will be needed. Of course, they can be replaced in between shots, but if you want to change in between frames then you must have easy access and ensure that the change is not too drastic. The replacement pieces have to be carefully matching in colour and have perfect registration.

Registration is the technique by which you ensure that the current shot lines up in every detail with the previous shot. In all forms of animation, it helps to refer back to previous images and any registration, whether it is pegs, charts or gauges, will help make sure the characters are orientated and that all the details line up.

3.14

Sleight of Hand: A Story in Stop-motion 2012

director
Michael Cusack
The creator in Michael Cusack's *Sleight of Hand* holding a spare mouthpiece, as the truth about his own existence dawns on him.

Rapid prototype printing

More recently, a process called rapid prototype printing, (used extensively in films like *Pirates!* and *ParaNorman*) allows dozens of replacement elements to be reproduced accurately, each with subtle differences. These replacements can provide more kinetic and exaggerated facial features than mechanics can. It provides the elastic qualities of clay animation but without the need for constant re-sculpting. Of course, the wider the range of movement required, the more replacements needed and… whoops, there goes the budget. But the results are amazing. Having a limited number of replacement heads still enables you to segue from one expression to the other but with less finesse.

Detailed, complex faces are fine if you can afford them, and have the time available to animate them, but don't always assume that a complex face is necessary for a good performance. Economy can lead to creative results, and good body-led performances from the puppet can often convey more than literal facial expressions. Many puppets and characters cope very well with simple replacement eyes and mouths and other economic techniques. Look at your film and ask how important facial expressions are, and whether there is a more interesting way to communicate.

Replacements are particularly efficient when an action has to be endlessly repeated, such as with marching toy soldiers. In this instance, it might work to have the whole body of such a toy soldier as a series of replacements but with an 'animatable' head moving independently, so that the viewer will not notice the repetition.

3.15

3.15

The Pirates! In an Adventure with Scientists! 2012

directors
Peter Lord and Jeff Newitt
Here, a basic pirate puppet has been deconstructed to show its many elements. More complex puppets had many more replacement mouth shapes.

Speed and economics

In addition to being useful for repetitious walk cycles, replacements can also be used for other effects such as a falling ball bouncing and changing briefly into a flattened shape. Replacements are certainly a much more practical and economical solution than building a ball with complex mechanics. The results can be glorious, but you should consider the planning involved, and the finesse needed so as not to show the difference between the sequential pieces.

My first encounter with replacements was on *Chorlton and the Wheelies* (1976–1979), a series designed to be produced quickly but effectively. Most of the characters were faces on wheels, making them easy to animate, as they couldn't fall over.

Animating walking characters is time consuming and so it was decided that Fenella, the wicked witch, would not walk either. Instead, she disappeared into the ground in a series of replacements and then reappeared elsewhere – the restricted budget of the show produced a suitably creative and fortuitously lively solution and one that fits the character and the pacing of the show.

These were pretty basic replacements and Fenella was limited to always disappearing in the same pose, but it was effective. In the same programme, the Wheelies' faces were replaceable with different and somewhat random expressions. There was no sense of moving from one expression to another; they simply changed, but it worked. Remember that necessity is the mother of invention and constraints of time and money can often lead to creative inspiration.

The puppets

3.16

3.16

Worms (aka Minhocas) 2013

directors
**Paolo Conti and
Arthur Nunes**
Junior, and his replacement
mouths, from *Minhocas*,
the first full-length Brazilian
stop-motion film.

George Pal

For George Pal and his Puppetoons
in the 1950s, replacements were
a trademark design trick, and many
of his puppets have very fluid faces,
full of stretch and squash. This
needed dozens of replacements,
all specifically and painstakingly
plotted for the particular sequence.

Many of Pal's short films feature
dozens of perfectly synchronized
soldiers; the repetition of their precise
movement would have defeated more
traditional stop-motion puppets. Have
a look at his spectacular *Rhythm in
the Ranks* (1941).

With puppets you can take away the nose in the design, and they still work. Remove the mouth as well and there's still life, but remove the eyes, and there's nothing. A single look from expressive eyes can make words redundant. Therefore, if you design a puppet with fixed eyes or no more than black dots then you are limiting that character's potential performance. Two black pinpricks can be just enough to give a puppet some life, giving the face a focus, and an outlet for expression, but the more detail in the eyes the better. The expression 'the eyes are the window to the soul' is hackneyed but true. If black dots are right for the design, then you will need to give that character particularly expressive body language.

Levels of subtlety

The type of eyes you use has an enormous impact on the way a character will perform and move. It should be one of the first decisions you make about a puppet. Fixed, generic eyes are honest and straightforward and allow little subterfuge, which may be appropriate for the story. If you want subtlety, black dots are unlikely to work. If you give the puppet realistic representations of human eyes, with enough whites to allow movement of the pupils, then you give the character a huge range of expression. Eyes slowly moving to one side immediately give some subtext and depth.

Any movement in the eyes suggests a thought process, and with moving eyes you can start to play with focus, and just as importantly, lack of focus. Add slowly blinking lids and the amount of expression is magnified enormously. Add eyebrows, and you have an unlimited range of expression. The puppet in *Tchaikovsky – An Elegy* had no animating facial features other than eyes, and maybe it is this almost blank canvas that has led audiences to see all manner of complex expressions in him.

If you go to the trouble and expense of creating a detailed puppet, make sure that you use it to its full potential. This means planning your storyboard and method of shooting to allow for shots that reveal the eye acting. Usually, a thought process and a subsequent movement will begin with the eyes focusing on something, showing the intent of a move to come. This then translates into the body.

Some schedules and budgets may not allow for complex eyes and eye acting, as struggling to keep eyes in focus and stopping puppets from making wayward glances and fiddling with replacement blinks all takes up valuable shooting time. There is, however, a magical moment as you place a puppet on the set and focus the eyes. Suddenly, with the eyes in focus and looking somewhere with deliberation, a lump of clay or brass armature and cloth becomes a character. It is an exciting transformation that still thrills me.

3.17

3.18

3.17

Tchaikovsky – An Elegy 2011

director
Barry JC Purves
Some thought process is
definitely going on with this
Tchaikovsky puppet, though
there is limited actual expression.
Photograph by Joe Clarke.

3.18

Life's a Zoo 2008

animator
Cuppa Coffee Studios
The characters from *Life's a Zoo*,
with their eyes suggesting some
clear intent and focus, but look
how the glasses rob the penguin
character of that intent.

Eye options

There are numerous ways to build eyes. Some puppets work with simple replacements, where the eye is literally poked out with a pin (not for the squeamish!) and replaced with a half shut or closed eye. Other puppets have glass or bead eyes set back in sockets and often held in place by magnets, either with a range of eyelids added or, luxuriously, mechanical lids that can close quickly or slowly. You can even replace eyes to allow for bigger or smaller irises, which has an enormous effect on how the character is perceived in terms of friendliness or hostility. Some puppets have simple stick-on eyes, or even a magnetic rubber pupil; on some the eyes are drawn on – the range is endless. A trick much favoured by stop-motion animators is to wet the eyes with glycerine. This brings them to life amazingly, giving unexpected highlights. Eyes are a time-consuming part of the animation process, but it is worth getting it right.

Alternatively, and depending on the character, you could hide the eyes behind sunglasses or a mask, which, while speeding up the animation, also brings a distinct feeling of coldness. This can actually be effective for characters with a darker nature, as nothing is revealed. A prime example of this is the unsettling effect achieved by replacing eyes with buttons on many of the characters in *Coraline*.

3.19

3.19

Playing Ghost 2011

director
Bianca Ansems
The mother, having her eyes painfully adjusted in *Playing Ghost*.

3.20

3.20

Madame Tutli-Putli 2007

directors
Chris Lavis and Maciek Szczerbowski
Madame Tutli-Putli and her amazing human eyes, matted onto a beautifully simple puppet.

Madame Tutli-Putli, a staggering film from 2007, has human eyes seamlessly matted onto a stop-motion puppet, and the effect is uncanny, disturbing and beautiful. It would have been too disturbing, though, if the face had been more realistic, but Madame Tutli-Putli is still clearly a puppet, with roughly sculpted face and hands, and a glorious fixed smudge of a mouth. The moist human eyes perfectly express the sense of dread and fear of her situation. There is no need for words. This technique was inevitably labour-intensive, but it is a remarkable and moving film.

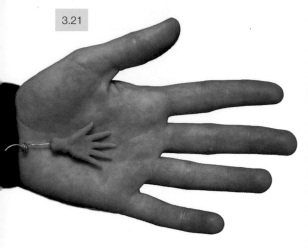

3.21

Hands are a major form of expression and need special consideration when developing a puppet. Traditionally, whether for reasons of economics or ease of drawing, cartoon characters often find themselves with just three fingers and a thumb. This shortcut is fine for drawings, but stop-motion puppets' fingers do have a practical prehensile purpose, as well as an aesthetic one, and it is desirable to have five digits if possible. It is not only much easier to hold props with four fingers and the all-important thumb, but the range of expression is considerably wider than with just three fingers and a thumb.

3.21

Out on the Tiles 2010

director
Anna Pearson
The scale of a puppet hand from Anna Pearson's *Out on the Tiles*.

If hands are important to the storytelling, too many facial close-ups will lose the hands. Likewise, if you give your character short arms, and a large belly, it is unlikely that the character will be able to link hands, again denying yourself much expression. Don't just design a character to look good. Consider how it is going to express itself.

3.22

Handy hints

The complex mechanics for expressive hands are expensive so do consider just how important and significant the hands are for your characters and film. It is well worth going through your script to decide just what will be required of your characters' hands and design them accordingly. Think about these ideas:

- Wire fingers can work well for simple puppets, but they have a limited life (often snapping) and they can seldom be straightened once bent.

- Silicon has excellent durability, but little will stick to it. Animators, therefore, often have to resort to pins, invisible thread and even superglue – all of which slow down the filming. Silicon can also develop tears when fingers are left in extreme positions for a long period. Silicon does, though, resemble flesh. Short silicon fingers will be difficult to bend, or can straighten after you have bent them.

- Clay, by its nature, can produce good chunky comedy hands, but long elegant fingers are hard to sustain; they simply fall to pieces or melt.

- During the filming process hands will suffer wear and tear and fingers will break, so you will need several pairs.

- Due to their small size hands will always be fiddly to animate, and animators dread the sound of a falling prop as it slips through a puppet's fingers. Placing small magnets embedded in the palms can help.

- Stop-motion characters are often based on animals, with paws that limit expression and grip. If you have animal characters think carefully about what their paws will need to do.

- Some characters with stylized hands still manage to be expressive through rhythm and pacing rather than actual articulation. The *Rick & Steve* (2007–2009) episodes are a great example as the characters are based on children's toys with fixed curved hands. This limitation becomes an essential feature of the animation, and is often referenced.

- With hands often trailing behind the movement of the arm, much attention is given to the wrist – make sure it is durable and flexible.

As with so many aspects of stop-motion, it's about the balance between the aesthetic and the practical. All this will test how much you enjoy working with small things; but then a gesture, beautifully expressed through an eloquent hand movement, is hugely satisfying.

3.22

In the Fall of Gravity 2008

animator
Ron Cole
These puppets have beautifully expressive hands. Hands can express enormous inner feeling when they are used thoughtfully, but insensitive, fussy treatment can distract from the performance.

There is no standard size for a stop-motion puppet. This is because the appropriate size is governed by the practicalities of the individual film, the studio – and the animator's hand. If the puppet is to have complicated mechanics in the head, it may help the **fabricators** if the puppets are larger than normal. If this is the case, then bear in mind that everything escalates once you decide to have larger puppets. For example, it will require larger sets, and therefore a larger space in the studio. The size of the puppet will also dictate the required strength of the joints – and very strong joints can be more difficult to animate.

Similarly, very small puppets are fiddly and awkward. It is often difficult to include the required detail in the sculpting and sufficiently fine texture in the costumes. Very small puppets can also sometimes necessitate animating with toothpicks when the animator's fingers simply aren't nimble enough. A practical size is usually dictated by simple ergonomics. Ask yourself whether you can you hold the puppet comfortably and steadily in one hand, and control it easily with the other. Most puppets end up somewhere around 22–30cm (9–12 inches). This scale should allow sufficiently detailed close-ups as well as controllable armatures. Some animators just can't manage to manipulate a small mouth, for example, without knocking the puppet, due to their own chunky fingers. Do think very carefully about the size implications of your puppets and how that will affect the sets and the studio space. It's all related.

Tip: Very large puppets

If a puppet gets too big, necessitating other animators or external manipulation, some animators worry about the lack of control. Much of the beauty of stop-motion is in its direct intimacy, with the puppets cradled in one hand. However, sometimes big puppets are necessary to a story. The large were-rabbit puppet in *The Curse of the Were-Rabbit* and the turtle in *Frankenweenie* needed more than one animator, and thus much extra co-ordination. The were-rabbit's features were controlled externally by discreet cables. This had the added benefit of leaving the fur untouched.

3.24

Next 1989

animator
Barry JC Purves
Myself, animating William Shakespeare, with an ergonomically pleasing puppet – with the now uncommon 35mm camera inhibiting the working space.

3.23

3.24

3.23

**Tales from the
Powder Room** 2002

animator
Darren Burgess
Darren Burgess animating a
character from his *Tales from the
Powder Room* – these puppets
are certainly a practical size.

Fabricators are a team of artists who look after all aspects of creating
puppets, from the detailed armatures to the tailored costumes and subtle
painting of the skins.

We've talked about clay, and the material is a great way to start animating as it is considerably cheaper than an armatured puppet. To animate with clay, however, you do need one skill that other animators do not: simply, you have to be able to sculpt. You also need an ability to keep a mental and physical image of the master shape in your head, and in your hands, as you resculpt the figure each frame. It would help to have a constant reference next to you as you shoot.

Clay is flexible and solid enough to act as its own armature with small moves, but more radical moves require re-sculpting and this fact has defeated many animators. The effort needed for sculpting can take away an animator's feeling for the movement. Due to the material, the characters have an inevitable chunkiness that is definitely part of their charm. You'll also find that most clay characters develop substantial feet, as that is the only way to make them stand up. If you are planning elegant or delicate characters for your film, clay may not be appropriate.

Scale, with clay, becomes an issue as the weight of the material can quickly become cumbersome with large puppets. Despite all these limitations, however, clay characters are also amazingly versatile and joyously hands-on; you can both feel and see the results of your animation. Clay has a wonderfully organic feel, rich in texture and ripe for transformations. If you want stretch and squash in your character, clay is exactly the right material.

Clay is a very physical form of animation, and the technique is an essential part of it. It is possible to have subtle movement with clay puppets, but this can be very time-consuming. Clay is fantastic for bold and brash statements and could be just the right material if liberated exaggeration is part of your puppet's performance. Scenes of contained introspection tend to be harder with clay. That said, although Adam Elliot's characters may not be hugely mobile (and this could be due to budgetary considerations or a reluctance to do too much sculpting) their stillness does give them a great pensive gravitas (see page 131).

Clay is also full of resonances with many cultures having myths of living clay characters such as the Golem, Prometheus creating living clay characters, and the Biblical Adam himself being born out of the clay. Certainly try it.

3.24

Faust 1994

animator
Jan Švankmajer
Clay used for a more disturbing effect. A character from Jan Švankmajer's dazzling *Faust*; a film full of many different bold techniques.

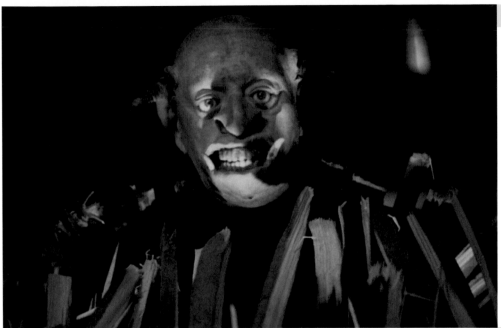

3.24

3.25

3.25

Beaver Creek 2008

animator
Ian Timothy
'Twigs' from Ian Timothy's
impressive *Beaver Creek* films.

Jan Švankmajer

Jan Švankmajer produces extraordinarily
visceral films. Not only does he push the
possibilities of clay, getting all manner of
meaning out of his transformations, he
also boldly mixes clay with objects, offal,
and literally anything. His breathtakingly
daring films are testament, again, that
the smallest object or the most unusual
material can be used to illustrate an idea
if that idea is good.

Armatures and clay

Armatures are sometimes used for clay puppets. This involves the clay being built up around the armature to form a flexible skin, sometimes even with preformed replacement mouths. This makes for a lighter puppet than using solid clay, and cuts out the need for repeated sculpting. However, it also means losing some of the stretch and squash capabilities of pure clay. For this reason, most puppets are solid clay, leading to a certain anatomical fluidity in the positioning of the joints. This is all part of the joy of working with clay and gives the characters a unique feel.

It is important to accept that fingerprints and variation of skin texture are an inseparable part of working with clay. This is something that should be enjoyed rather than hidden. Clay animation is accessible and there is never any doubt that its characters have existed as part of the real world. With CG getting more and more astounding each day, it's satisfying that a mere and obvious lump of clay can still move audiences and provoke laughter.

Recommended viewing

Have a look at the Gnome King sequences in *Return to Oz* (1985) for some imaginative use of clay animation. Here, the technique of clay is totally appropriate for the character of a living mountain, constantly transforming. This was produced by Will Vinton Productions – Will's earlier short film, *The Great Cognito* (1982), features a string of remarkable and very detailed transformations, and showed clay's potential. Aardman Animation continues to push clay animation into all areas of imaginative sophistication, from the joyous Morph short films to full-length Wallace and Gromit feature films.

The puppets

3.26

3.26

**Mona Lisa Descending
a Staircase** 1992

director
Joan C. Gratz
Artists such as Joan Gratz use
clay for painting, relishing the
transformations and textures
that clay offers. Have a look at
her beautiful film, *Mona Lisa
Descending a Staircase*.

If you find puppets either too literal or too expensive, but you still want to enjoy the tactile nature of stop-motion, there are many other options. Two are sand and cut-outs, but don't think there is a limit to what can be animated. The techniques and tricks of stop-motion, of manipulating objects by hand, still apply whether the objects are tiny grains of sand, or hundreds of Post-it notes on a wall, or large chunks of scrap. The important idea is that you are using your hands to directly control the material. Anything that can be moved in a real space is capable of being part of an animated film, and producing exciting images.

Have a look at the films from Pes, particularly *The Deep* (2010), where everyday tools are transformed into extraordinary and beautiful undersea characters.

3.27

3.27

Una Furtiva Lagrima 2012

director
Carlo Vogele
This hauntingly lyrical film features a real fish, bought from the local market, lip-synching amazingly accurately to an operatic piece by Donizetti and Bellini. Carlo is a Pixar animator and the hands-on approach must have made a satisfying, if somewhat smelly, lo-tech change.

3.28

3.28

Day Shift 2012

director
Ian Timothy
Ian Timothy's *Day Shift* is proud to show its characters' settings are made of everyday objects, as they are appropriate to the narrative. Again, don't assume the basic nature of the puppets prohibits a nuanced performance.

The puppets

Sand

The work of Vera Neubauer, Caroline Leaf and Joanna Priestley are all good examples of limited resources being used with a great deal of creativity. They certainly prove that it is not essential to have fully armatured puppets to produce powerful animation. All three use sand and various found objects to produce some beautifully textured films with a wonderful graphic quality. Joanna Priestley's films use objects to produce very poignant and resonant collages. Caroline Leaf, in films such as *The Owl who Married a Goose: An Eskimo Legend* (1976) and *The Metamorphosis of Mr Samsa* (1978), uses sand in combination with a light box, and the results are subtle and quite unique, mixing the graphic qualities of drawing with more dimensional work full of texture and relief. Vera Neubauer's work, in films such as *Wheel of Life* (1996), has a more direct rawness and vitality, drawing directly into sand on the beach alongside flotsam and jetsam. Both uses of sand are evocative and startling, and for all the visible technique still manage to communicate something profound and moving. Another recent film, *Bottle* (2010), by Kirsten Lepore showed a tragic long-distance romance between a real snowman and a sand figure endeavouring to meet across a raging river.

3.29

3.29

The Owl who Married a Goose: An Eskimo Legend 1976

animator
Caroline Leaf
Here, Caroline Leaf works on her sand film *The Owl who Married a Goose*. The use of a light box turns the imagery into something very graphic and beautiful, almost a drawing but with tangible texture.

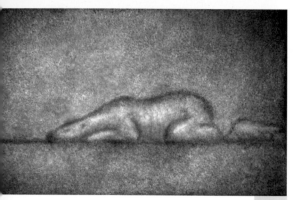

3.30   3.30

Bear with Me 2008

animator
Uriah Naeh
Rather than sand, this film
uses sea salt on glass, lit from
underneath; it was created
by Uriah Naeh at the Bezalel
Academy of Arts and Design
in Jerusalem. The results are
sublime and delicate.

Cut-outs

Cut-outs are another unique form of
animation, and the works of Lotte Reiniger,
Michel Ocelot and Yuriy Norshteyn show how
extraordinarily rich and delicate this technique
can be. It's still a very tactile technique,
and once you have created the puppets
you don't have to keep resculpting them,
though a single character may have various
elements that are changeable according to
its movements.

To work with cut-outs you will need an acute
eye for how a character works as a silhouette,
and how movement works in profile. Cut-
outs mixed with a multi-plane camera set-up
literally add another dimension, and though
computers are able to replicate such an effect
easily, there are still effective stop-motion
examples today.

It's a great joy to animate with cut-outs
because you have all the pleasure of touching
and manipulating puppets, but you don't
have to worry about gravity or puppet joints.
Of course there are other challenges; if you
don't have the right paper, the characters
can curl up. Fingerprints on the layers of
glass can slow production too. You also need
extremely steady hands to move the paper
pieces with precision. Animators often push
the characters around with toothpicks as
sometimes fingers are just too clumsy and
maybe too sweaty, sticking to the paper.
However, this is a very economical, personal
and intimate form of animation, which is still a
hands-on experience, and the results can give
beautiful movement and gorgeous images.

The puppets

3.31

3.31

Being Bradford Dillman 2011

director
Emma Burch
Emma Burch's exquisite and unsettling film *Being Bradford Dillman* uses a fascinating combination of jointed cut-out flat figures set against miniature backgrounds. Some of the scenes in this film were achieved through using the multi-plane system, and mixed with detailed props.

3.32

The puppets

Tip: Matching ideas and techniques

When writing your script, constantly ask yourself whether your favoured technique can realize your ideas. If it can't, it's probably easier to revise the technique than the ideas, though often in animation they are so tightly knitted together it is hard to separate them. However, it would be wrong to force an inappropriate technique onto an idea if you have to compromise that idea.

3.32

Roots of the Hidden 2012

director
Elizabeth Marie Sevenoaks
Another novel film using cut-outs is Lizzie Sevenoaks' atmospheric *Roots of the Hidden*, with flat figures made of pierced and laser-cut basswood. This atmospheric, multi-layered film hints at the early silhouette puppets of Lotte Reiniger and Javanese shadow puppets.

Recommended viewing

It's a Bird (1930) directed by Harold L. Muller, is a highly ingenious short film that includes a stop-motion bird eating its way through the contents of a scrapyard. The bird then lays an egg, which hatches and grows into a full-scale car. All this is achieved complete with camera moves and a live-action character watching. The same story could now be shown relatively easily with CG, but knowing the patience, concentration and memory required to place the items with such accuracy makes it more captivating. Again, understanding the technique is part of the pleasure of the film.

3.33

Les Trois Inventeurs 1980

Animator
Michel Ocelot
This exquisite still shows the delicate but very textural paper cut-outs, and the importance of a strong clear silhouette.

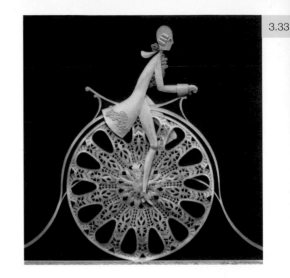

3.33

3.34

The Tale of Sir Richard 2006

Animator
Peter Dodd
Peter Dodd's *The Tale of Sir Richard* used flat shapes that rested on the glass but also had relief on the upper surface. This film beautifully combines heavily textured, sculpted replacement pieces on different layers of glass. The effective results have a feel of puppets but without the expense of complicated armatures or the problems of gravity and enormous budgets. It also retains the joy of the tactile process, and the movement has an elastic anatomy hard to achieve in jointed puppets.

3.34

The puppets

Getting ready

With the script and characters clear, start to storyboard and design bearing in mind the resources you have. Can you use the camera, the colours, the design, and the sound to help get the story over more economically? Does every element reveal something about the story and characters?

● Time the storyboard, or make an animatic if possible. Does it feel rushed or are there too many shots?

● Have you allowed time to let the important moments read? Or are there too many close-ups, perhaps?

● Record any dialogue, and break it down into frames, but is the dialogue adding anything that can't be done visually?

● Find a music track, and play that against the board or animatic. Does the music create the right mood and pace?

● Make a list of all the puppets, props, costumes, lighting and so forth, that you will need. Plan a schedule for the puppet and set building, and a shooting order.

In the next chapter we'll explore the practicalities of making a one-minute film...

4.1

Here, we'll look at all the preparation that is necessary for an easy shoot, and what sort of problems and pleasures you'll encounter on a film set. The process at this stage of film-making is very different from any other form of animation, with much more physicality involved. Detailed preparation before shooting will save so many problems later and is an essential stage to go through.

4.1

Mary and Max 2009

animator
Adam Elliot
This sums up everything that is glorious about stop-motion; enjoying all the elements of design, texture, lighting, colour, depth, detail and character to produce something very stylized but instantly credible and recognizable. Every element is working in harmony with the others and the purpose of every element has been considered.

Easy-to-use apps have given the chance for so many people to get involved with animation. It has literally become 'set up – move the character – click and playback' and there it is on YouTube minutes later. Little money is involved and you can be more casual and spontaneous. Apart from anything, you can get a cheap taste of animation before pursuing further projects involving greater precision, more detail and more expense.

A professional stop-motion set-up is somewhat different, for as soon as a film goes into production suddenly more people become involved, each with a specific role, all overseen by the producer. The producer makes sure that the right people are doing the right things on time and within the right budget, whilst keeping the many different, fragmented units all working together as one. The producer also acts as a facilitator, allowing the director to realize their vision of the film whenever it is logistically possible. Producers have the pressure whilst directors have the pleasure.

Similarly, one of the director's key roles is to keep all of the different departments working towards the same artistic end. The director must ensure that every decision is in keeping with the spirit and style of the film, and that every element is used to its fullest potential; that the **semiotics** of the film all work as one. The director gives a film the necessary unified vision, and thorough preparation is essential in achieving this. The necessity of working in a group applies to similar set-ups at colleges and universities.

4.2

4.2

Friendly Fire 2008

animator
Andreas Kaiser
An early mood sketch from *Friendly Fire*, which suggests a look for the finished film, and helps everyone involved know what the director is hoping to achieve.

4.3

Miss Todd 2013

director
Kristina Yee
Two of the many detailed sets for Kristina Yee's *Miss Todd*, designed for easy access of camera and for the animator to be able to reach the cut-out character.

4.3

Semiotics is the study of signs and symbols and their use or interpretation.

Once the initial narrative and thematic ideas have been established, the next stage is the development of a script. Once the script has been completed (and that does make this part of the process sound unfeasibly easy – it's not), the design process will continue and lead to the creation of a full storyboard. If there is sufficient budget, this will be further developed into full pre-visualizations and the story reel or animatic.

The main purpose of a storyboard is to provide a practical and accurate idea of how the finished film will turn out, and how each shot will fit into the overall picture. It is about camera angles and film grammar, which is important for the camera operator and set dressers to know in advance. Due to the number of people generally involved in a film, the production can get fragmented – the storyboard is the vital common constant point of reference for everyone involved. Even if you're performing all these roles yourself, you will still need the same clear pre-production planning.

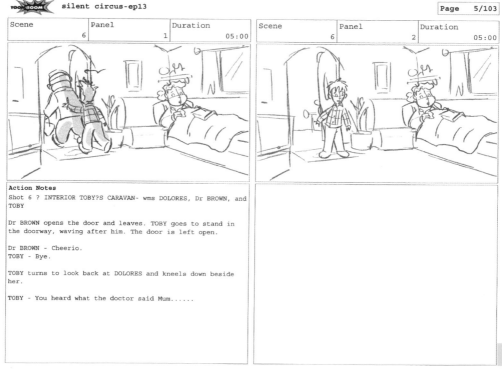

silent circus-ep13 | Page 5/103

Scene	Panel	Duration
6	1	05:00

Scene	Panel	Duration
6	2	05:00

Action Notes

Shot 6 ? INTERIOR TOBY?S CARAVAN- wms DOLORES, Dr BROWN, and TOBY

Dr BROWN opens the door and leaves. TOBY goes to stand in the doorway, waving after him. The door is left open.

Dr BROWN - Cheerio.
TOBY - Bye.

TOBY turns to look back at DOLORES and kneels down beside her.

TOBY - You heard what the doctor said Mum......

4.4

Animatics and pre-visualizations

Usually, when the director is happy with the storyboard, they are edited into an animatic the length of the proper film, using approximate timings, with basic sound, camera moves and music. This is where it becomes apparent what is working well and what needs changing. Spending time in careful preparation at the beginning of the film-making process will mean that the later more expensive studio time is well managed.

Sometimes you may have the luxury of pre-visualizations (previz), which are roughly animated digital recreations of the eventual film. There are basic virtual sets blocked out and rudimentary characters. The director is able to move the camera through this CG world looking for the perfect angle. The director must be aware, though, that whilst a digital camera can get into the smallest or oddest of places, a real-world camera has physical restrictions.

4.4

Toby's Travelling Circus 2012–

director
Barry JC Purves
producers
Richard Randolph and Chris Bowden
Storyboards, by their very nature, are static and may need several drawings to convey the important action of a scene. You'll find it easier if you work with one shot per page of the board, as it becomes easier to see what effect the removal or addition of a shot will have, and how shots then sit next to each other. In this way, your board will be practical and adaptable.

The purpose of all this is to ensure that everyone involved has a clear, shared understanding of the key elements required for the finished film. Through these various processes the director can anticipate what will work and what should be cut. This thorough preparation avoids making costly impromptu decisions on the set. Stop-motion is so time-consuming that we really can't afford to shoot any more than is needed for the finished film or to let anyone stand around problem solving.

Many storyboards are drawn by extremely talented artists with vivid imaginations. If these artists don't have an accurate and detailed knowledge of the limitations of the sets, or the construction of the puppets, it's all too easy to draw boards full of wild angles, dynamic perspectives and exaggerated expressions that can't be practically recreated in the studio. Basically, just draw only what a camera, with its various lenses, can see. Similarly, a writer may make an important point with a detailed description of a character's expression, but this is not much help if the real puppet only has two fixed painted eyes.

You will save yourself a great deal of time and trouble by working out the logistics of each scene during the writing and preparation process rather than trying to figure it out when you are on set. Even when filming spontaneously with a camera app, preparation will help you get better results.

Building sets is a hugely appealing aspect of stop-motion and gives people great satisfaction, harking back to playing with dolls' houses, train sets and model building as a child. There always has been, and always will be, something inherently satisfying about standing in front of a solid miniature world. If you have an eye for detail and texture, stop-motion is definitely for you.

Unlike with CG or drawn films, a stop-motion set has to accommodate many important requirements. They must allow access for the animator, as well as the cameras and lights. They must also be sufficiently stable to withstand animators stretching in and leaning on the surfaces during every frame; not allowing anything to wobble or sag or bend during the shot. Furniture and props are usually secured to the set with sticky wax, hot glue, or magnets, to stop any unnecessary movement. Even the changing temperatures of the lights can cause a set to buckle. Even more challengingly, a set designer must make what is essentially a flat tabletop look like a convincing interior or epic vista.

4.5

4.6

4.6

Head Over Heels 2012

director
Timothy Reckart
A still from the finished film, where husband and wife Walter and Madge have grown apart; he lives on the floor and she lives on the ceiling.

4.5

Head Over Heels 2012

director
Timothy Reckart
The beautifully detailed set of Tim Reckart's National Film and Television School (UK) graduation film, *Head Over Heels*, and the clutter beyond the frame.

Tip: Thinking ahead

When you are writing the story, drawing the storyboard, or working on the digital previz, it's all too easy to forget the realities of stop-motion. A script can easily describe a scene of wild, energetic choreography, but bringing that to life is much more difficult. While you should never rein in your imagination when writing, it is important to constantly be aware that you are dealing with physical characters, and the script and storyboard must reflect this. Don't forget that surmounting these physical problems is part of the fun for both the maker and the audience.

Scale and false perspective

All manner of theatrical tricks such as gauzes, false perspectives, and clever painting go some way to achieving a grand scale, but it has to be said that CG can create the most amazing and spectacular landscapes, certainly beyond anything that can be built practically in a normal studio and with restricted budgets. If your film is all about sweeping landscapes or complex cityscapes, do think about using CG to supplement the real sets. CG can also add shafts of light, atmosphere, weather and a whole range of elements not feasible on the studio floor. Alternatively, you may want to film your puppet characters against a green screen and composite them into a CG environment. This is certainly a practical solution, but it is often not as much fun as creating real sets and working with techniques such as false perspective. Digital photography makes finessing, correcting and embroidering your images so much easier, but then some directors like the pure untouched image. I confess, I am one of those.

If you do choose to rely on false perspectives to help create a sense of scale, then you must think carefully about all the angles that you will use. The illusion can be easily destroyed and maintaining it requires careful planning in the storyboards. To make it easier, stop-motion sets are usually built with a 'front' – this not only helps orientate the viewer, but it helps practically with all the rigging and the lighting. If you have a set that will be shot from 360 degrees, all the walls will need to be removable and probably the lighting changed for each set-up. This will require more space and time on the studio floor.

4.7

4.8

4.7

The Man Who Was Afraid of Falling 2013

director
Joseph Wallace
A simple, effective use of false perspective, with small trees that are out of focus in the background.

4.9

4.8

Goutte d'Or 2013

director
Christophe Peladan
An image from *Goutte d'Or*,
inserting stop-motion puppets
into a mostly CG environment.

4.9

**Sleight of Hand: A Story in
Stop-motion** 2012

director
Michael Cusack
An image from the set of *Sleight
of Hand*. In one sequence, the
camera seemingly travelled
360 degrees around the main
character, though in this instance,
it was the set and the lights that
moved on a revolving platform.
This required sturdy sets, much
planning with the lighting and
easily removable walls.

Aspect ratios

When designing sets it's essential to consider the aspect ratio that the film will be shot in, and to try to map out every composition in advance. Films for television were traditionally shot in a 4:3 ratio, which was great for close-ups of single talking heads, but now the shape is usually 16:9, which more closely resembles the human visual field. Such a shape can allow two close-up heads to be conversing and reacting to each other in the same frame, without the need for the usual cutting back and forth. I enjoy two shots as the listener can be as important as the speaker. This obviously affects your film grammar. Also, as movement is crucial to animation, the shape allows a full figure to move about the frame with sufficient space, without necessarily moving the camera.

The shape can be even more extreme with animation produced for cinema. Widescreen is certainly dynamic, with standard ratios between 1.66: 1, 1.85: 1 and 2.40:1. Try staging a simple two-way conversation in the different ratios and see how that affects the storytelling and the number of shots needed. The oblong is a more pleasing shape, and makes a better use of space, and more striking compositions.

Credibility

If a set is too clean and flat, or the textures are too large, then it can easily disrupt the illusion of scale. Texture, stop-motion's great friend, can help mitigate this effect. Introducing some essential weathering to the sets can also help. Sets need to look lived-in, as though they have existed before the camera arrived, and you'll be surprised what a difference a bit of shading in corners or the odd scratch can make. The same applies to costumes. As always, it's the little unexpected touches and imperfections that make a set and a character credible to the viewer.

Animators usually prefer working on real sets, where we can respond to the environment and introduce tiny but telling details. Working in a green-screen vacuum is exactly that – a vacuum. It's harder to feel part of the scene, and to some extent the animation could become a disconnected layer. Time and time again we come back to enjoying stop-motion because it is all there right in front of us and we can touch it, and our characters can react to the real set around them.

4.10

Electreecity 2008

animators
Sarah Davison and Sarah Duffield-Harding
A beautifully stylized, simple and imaginative set. This scene makes creative use of texture, and gives a familiar image of a tree a fresh perspective.

4.10

4.11

4.11

Tchaikovsky – An Elegy 2011

director
Barry JC Purves
Entrances through doors make a great impact, but animating characters coming through them is certainly tricky. The author struggling with Tchaikovsky. Photograph by Joe Clarke.

Tip: Doors

Remember that there will be elements on the set that will need to be animated at specific times, such as doors, but for the rest of the scene they need to be rock solid. Magnets can help with this or small hinges that can be tensioned. Nothing ruins a shot more than a character walking towards a door, and the door twitching before it is opened, caused by an animator's clumsiness – walking a character through a door is notoriously difficult. Everything has to be fixed solidly to the set and yet still be free to move as necessary. Solving this requires ingenuity and to enjoy stop-motion it certainly helps to enjoy this kind of problem solving.

Character and style

As every single item has to be created from scratch, why not liberate yourself from reproducing reality and enjoy giving the sets character and style? Sets, like all the other elements of your film, should contribute to and reflect the overarching story, characters and themes. When you are designing, try to create a whole new credible world for the characters, where everything works seamlessly together. Don't automatically design around human proportions. Study your characters and design around them. Much of the success of the *Wallace and Gromit* films depends on the details in the sets: some are only apparent in repeated viewings.

Consider how much the dog bones on Gromit's wallpaper say about him. Just as there is often a visual shorthand for puppets (such as haughty characters being portrayed by tall, spiky puppets) so the colour and shapes used in sets can immediately flavour the stories they tell. It may help the viewer if you give each location its own visual identity and palette. Of course, however fanciful you get with the sets, it's essential that the characters stand out clearly in front of them. The sets support the characters, not the other way round.

Life beyond the frame

Although most sets are based on a tabletop, it's helpful to suggest life continuing not just either side of the frame, but also above and below it, and outside windows. While designing for the camera, don't forget to allow room for your characters, especially characters with significant shadows, to walk out of shot. This is particularly helpful when you are dealing with vehicles. Too often I've animated a car to the edge, and run out of set, with half remaining in shot. Again, these issues should be considered carefully during pre-production planning and through working with your designer.

Any details built into the set (such as leaves or papers on the floor, or swinging doors) that can react to characters as they pass by can be extremely effective, helping plant the characters tangibly in their world. Adding elements in post-production, such as mists or moving clouds or shadows, also helps. In my film *Tchaikovsky*, hundreds of rose petals fell to the floor. As Tchaikovsky walked through them these flurried up around him. Some were CG; others were paper petals moved along the floor.

4.12

Compost Corner 2012

director
Westley Wood
This set from *Compost Corner* is a comfortable height and designed to allow easy access for animator and camera.

Foregrounds

If your set contains a foreground element, such as a lawn with long grass or flowers, this will add great depth but may be a nightmare to work with. You will have to lean over the foreground for each frame, probably knocking the flowers or rustling the grass. Spraying the grass with hairspray may help, as would making the flowers very rigid. However, if you are shooting on digital it might be easier to treat the foreground piece as a separate element. Shoot it with a piece of blue screen behind ahead of the shot, and then remove it. It can then be replaced in post-production. It's even more effective if you soften the focus of the foreground piece in post, as that will increase the illusion of depth. This technique can solve problems but does prevent the animator from seeing the complete picture and limits the use of camera moves, although you could film a matching foreground move as a separate pass.

Set height

The most convenient height for a set is usually level with the animator's waist. This height will normally minimize the physical strain caused by repetitive bending and twisting. While considering the height of the set do make sure that the camera equipment is suitably adaptable, and that the camera can sit in a position appropriate for the viewpoint of the film. I worked on one low set where the unthinking cameraman shot everything from his eye level, rather than at the eye level of the characters in the set, giving a God-like perspective not intended in the script. Ask yourself whether, in every shot, the camera is subjective or objective.

A puppet in a gloriously well-fitting and detailed costume can be very expressive and reveal so much about the character and story, but as with all things, think what the costumes will contribute. The costumes will be touched in every frame, and they need to be designed accordingly to prevent constant twitching. One solution is to have double-sided tape to stick the costume to the puppet, or they can be loosely sewn to the skin. However, clothes must be able to move freely with the puppet, not restricting the joints. Costumes must also allow access to the armature so that the animator can adjust their tension when necessary. The seams that allow this access should be as invisible as possible, or you can use tricks such as removable pockets.

Another effect of touching the costume every frame is that, however clean your hands, they inevitably become dirty, or certain fabrics will 'bobble'. Shooting out of sequence makes this more noticeable, so think carefully before you give your main character a pristine white, woolly outfit!

It's also worth bearing in mind that you are unlikely to be able to maintain much detail, shape or finesse in a clay costume, as this will have to be resculpted or touched up more times than it is worth.

4.13

The Gravedigger's Tale 2013

director/animator
Min Young Oh
The beautifully textured and detailed costume from Min Young Oh's *The Gravedigger's Tale*.

4.14

Oh Willy... 2012

directors
Emma De Swaef and Marc James Roels
Costumes are not just something that cover the puppets – they can help the narrative and characters, but always think of the practical issues involved. In the beautiful and melancholy *Oh Willy...*, the design concept was about woolly fabric, with all the sets and costumes and skin being made from a loose, hairy felt, and lit to make the most of every strand. The movement caused by the animator's hand was actively encouraged.

4.13

4.14

4.15

4.16

4.15

Tomorrow 2010

animator
Bob Lee
Thanks to the detail and
distressing, the costume in
Bob Lee's film *Tomorrow* looks
credible, and gives the character
an immediate history.

4.16

Tchaikovsky – An Elegy 2011

director
Barry JC Purves
The author giving Tchaikovsky's
wired jacket a flapping movement
as he conducts. Photograph by
Joe Clarke.

Fabric and shoes

Nothing betrays the scale of a puppet more than fabric. The printed fabric that looks delicate when used for a full-size human outfit will often look like thick, rough hessian when used on a miniature puppet seen in close-up on screen. It is important to carefully select a fabric that will work at the scale of your film. If your fabric is too lightweight, then it is unlikely to have enough weight to hang properly. Clever tailoring and wiring can help here, but if it is too heavy it will stick out stiffly. It's likely that any fabric you buy will have to be dyed, or printed, or given some help to make it look appropriate. As with the sets, weathering and distressing the costumes will help them look lived in. On a large shoot, you'll need duplicates of the main characters' costumes, so be careful to make a design that can be reproduced. Details such as feathers and fur will need a lot of care to ensure that they are in scale with the rest of the film.

Shoes are an essential part of any costume, unless the whole film is in close-up, but they are also something of a problem. Every puppet has to be attached to the set in some way and whatever method you choose will affect the design of the shoes. If you are using magnets, you'll need to incorporate a flat metal base, which will be awkward if you are thinking of high heels. If you are using tie-downs, consider how the screw will work with the shoe. As always, it's important to accommodate the various technical issues of stop-motion into your designs. Overcoming these challenges can be a joy in itself.

Life and movement

Costumes have to suit the characters, and they have to look appropriate in terms of scale and texture. Just as importantly, they should also be used to help the movement of the character. Everything in animation is about giving the suggestion of life and movement, and costumes are no different. When a stop-motion character is animated running, their clothes will not naturally trail behind them and so the animators must create this effect. Even something as simple as a wired animatable scarf flapping behind a running character will help give an illusion of momentum, although it is extra work to animate.

As you develop each scene, think how costume might help or hinder the illusion you are creating. If the scene involves dozens of ballroom dancers packed together, just reaching the puppets will be hard enough. Also, dresses are notoriously difficult to work with as they have to be lifted for access to the legs, and then repositioned, hopefully in the same place. For a ball scene you might have to create a very different method of animating the puppet, perhaps using solid dresses, or rigs that rise and fall, or you might have to shoot it without showing the legs (which would be sad).

When a set is prepared and the camera is in place, it is usually too late to make changes to the puppets, costumes, props or sets. Therefore, another vital element of your film that must be decided during pre-production is the colour scheme. This is where CG has a distinct advantage as a few buttons can easily change the tones, hues and colours of a whole scene. In stop-motion we can adjust colours somewhat in post, but it is preferable to think through and cement your vision of the film early on.

Once the sets, puppets and costumes have been made there is no room for change. This should lead to a cohesive design, even for films that take years to produce, as all the key decisions are made at the start. Of course things inevitably develop, but if all the designed elements of your film work together they strengthen the integrity of the whole, leaving the main spontaneity to come from the performances.

Colour palettes

Colour can contribute much more than just pleasing aesthetics – particular colours can produce various emotional responses in the audience. This is especially important in children's films, where bright colours are usually required. Like texture, which we enjoy so much in stop-motion, detailed colour comes easily in this medium. Puppets can be painted with an endless range of colour and gradations and textures. However, as with costumes, the puppet will be touched every frame and pale colours will show any marks easily. The ivory waistcoat for my Tchaikovsky puppet became stained through daily contact, but in this instance, we shot sequentially and the progressive staining goes unnoticed. Avoid, too, fine detail that could get smudged through constant handling. Unless you have the schedule to constantly clean the puppets, do think carefully before choosing a very light palette. You will also need to work very closely with the designers to make sure that the colours of the puppets stand out against the backgrounds.

Any puppet and set will be subject to wear and tear during a long shoot, so try to find colour schemes that can be matched. When thinking of the colour palette, do work with the lighting team, making sure your specifically chosen colours don't end up in shadow or bathed in light that kills the colour. As always, make these decisions at the start.

4.17

4.17

Madame Tutli-Putli 2007

directors
**Chris Lavis and
Maciek Szczerbowski**

The convincing, detailed costume and props worn by Madame Tutli-Putli don't betray their scale. They complement the detailed and weathered set, which must have contained some ingenious access points for the animators.

4.18

4.18

L'Oiseau 2009

animator
Samuel Yal

Two stills from Samuel Yal's *L'Oiseau* using wonderfully bold colour schemes and strikingly uncluttered compositions.
© Double Mètre Animation

4.19

4.19

Stanley Pickle 2011

director
Vicky Mather
The unsettling colour palette
and details from *Stanley Pickle*,
combining pixilation and stop-
motion to disturbing effect.
Pixilation is a technique where
real people are manipulated a
frame at a time, often doing the
seemingly impossible, giving a
movement close in style and feel
to stop-motion. Drew Caiden
plays Stanley.

Practical puppets

So you are constructing the two characters, but can they do what you want them to? Spend some time just holding the puppets, looking at them, and ask yourself the following questions:

● Do the puppets feel good in your hand?

● Can you move them and do they hold their position? If not, play with the tension of the joints.

● How will they stand up on the set?

● Will they survive a minute's filming?

● Can they hold any props?

● Do they need costumes and will the costumes allow sufficient movement?

● Will they cope with a close-up?

● Can they walk and can you reach them at the various places of the set?

● What facial expressions are necessary?

● Do the puppets have suitably expressive eyes that can keep their focus?

It's also worth carefully considering the capabilities of the set:

● Does it allow enough access for animators, cameras and lights?

● Is it sturdy enough?

● Can you reach where you need to?

In the next chapter, we'll get started on the filming…

5.1

In this penultimate chapter, we will look at how all of the technical elements involved with stop-motion affect the storytelling and the film itself and how they are just as important as the animation.

Since we have to create absolutely everything from scratch, it's important to make the most of every single element, letting them contribute to the film, rather than just being an afterthought, or mere decoration, or simply architecture. Try to give every cut, every framing, every piece of music some resonance to the overall narrative and theme. Animation is not solely about moving characters; it is about storytelling, and every element can help that story to be told.

5.1

Sleight of Hand: A Story in Stop-motion 2012

director
Michael Cusack
A beautifully detailed prop camera, used in the film to give the creative process a larger resonance.

Once you have moved a real object in real space, although it is captured as a digital still image, the preceding pose has gone forever. With drawn and computer animation the previous moves still exist very clearly on paper or in the computer, and the subsequent move can be adjusted and fine-tuned accordingly. Your reaction to this element of imprecision is probably a good reflection of how well you are suited to stop-motion.

Some animators feel much happier and safer when their animation is backed up by mathematics, with the chance of several, progressively more subtle takes and with the opportunity to actually work out a move before doing it. For some, however, mathematics gets in the way of performance, and the hand memory (and muscle memory) and, most important of all, instinct, are all that is needed for good animation. For many stop-motion animators our love of the medium is about that abstract quality – performance – and no amount of precise measurements and refining can make good animation if there is no natural instinct for performance, storytelling and acting. If you feel daunted by the idea of instinctive performance, then stop-motion, without its technical safety net, may not be right for you. But if you find this hint of the unknown exciting then you might have found the right medium to tell your story.

The appeal of this raw approach may mean that you get frustrated when technology comes between you and the performance. However, the technology of playback systems certainly does make life much easier. Animators are sometimes nervous about tinkering too much with puppets in between the frames, and usually take a big breath before removing a puppet from the set for some maintenance necessary to save a shot. They are worried about breaking some through line of action and never getting the puppet back into position. Getting the puppet back in the exact position is a question of a highly developed muscle memory, a few surface gauges, outrageous fortune and instinct. Playbacks of the preceding frame, especially with 'onion skins' that allow you to see the previous frame layered with the existing shot, have made this much easier. Many playback systems can enable you to delete a rogue frame, or even go back and insert a new frame. Dots and lines can be drawn on the screen as guides for various movements, but all these tricks are about making sure the frame is right before you move on. They should not get in the way of the performance itself.

5.2

The Maker 2012

director
Christopher Kezelos
Christopher Kezelos at work on
the cramped set of *The Maker*.

The camera

There is something very comforting about having a camera on a stop-motion set. We are the only animators that get to see one, and it reinforces the idea that stop-motion is a performance, and that there is an audience to witness this performance. Other animators must feel a sense of detachment as they work on their camera-less light boxes and computers. For the stop-motion animator, the camera is a continual presence, and we should be respectful of it. It gives a focus to the proceedings, and the sound of a shutter clicking, even a digital shutter, is an essential part of the process.

The physicality of stop-motion means that the camera can be both a blessing and a curse as it can get in the way. For this reason, stop-motion animators develop an odd body language as they work twisted around the camera – leading to many aching backs. Many older films were shot on glorious but awkward and bulky 35mm cameras, and the building of the sets had to take into consideration the presence of, and access needed by, the camera. The introduction of small digital still cameras has made animators' lives so much easier. The tiny camera can go right into the sets and into awkward angles that were never previously possible. This has had an enormous impact on the way we tell our stories, and is something that must be considered at the storyboarding stage.

Many traditional animators miss the imperfections and the forgiving, warm richness of real film, though few miss the bulky cameras on set, nor the tricky unloading of the precious film, and the wait for it to be developed. Digital is so sharp and crisp, although it's also quick to expose any flaws. The size of digital cameras, the instant feedback they can provide, the extraordinary potential for manipulation of the images, and the ease of sharing the footage make the whole process more accessible to beginners and those with limited resources. We are also seeing many kinetic films shot on phones, with animation released from the controlled environment of the studios.

Physical limitations

In stop-motion we cannot avoid the fact that there must be a camera in front of the set, and any camera moves have to be animated frame by frame. This raises problems of access to the set, shadows caused by their movements, and the space taken up by tracking equipment. All of this is undeniably challenging. However, as is so often the case with stop-motion, developing inventive solutions to these problems is incredibly satisfying.

Camera moves have been slowly introduced during the history of stop-motion. At first, the shots were set up like a theatre stage, with the characters moving within the static frame. Later, a few handheld moves with imprecise increments appeared. This led to the camera being placed on tracks, which allowed it to travel sideways following a puppet, or even track into a set. Next was the introduction of complicated and cumbersome motion-control rigs, which enabled the camera to move on several axes. These were initially manual, and often highly ingenious, but the introduction of computers to the process permitted

5.3

the camera to repeat the movements with precision. It is now possible to achieve several passes accurately, increasing the potential for overlaying special effects.

Cameras can now be relatively mobile, but the planning of camera moves is time-consuming, and they must be meticulously plotted beforehand. This can make the animator feel that they must keep up with the camera rather than the camera following the movement of the characters. This cramps the animation, as the animator has to make sure that the character is at a given mark at a given frame to be in the shot and in focus; thus killing some spontaneity. However, if the schedule allows, the cameras can be choreographed to follow the action, as in the brilliant *Madame Tutli-Putli*, where the effect is of live-action camerawork, with all its imperfections and random energy.

Smaller digital cameras and camera phones are much easier to use, but even so, any camera move involves extra work, and has to be shot in single frames to work. This will conflict with any animation shot in doubles frames, and give an unpleasant strobing effect.

5.3

Viv & Mandy in the Big Clean Up 2012

director
Daniel James
Student Daniel James' characters Viv and Mandy on set, well the floor, with all the necessary associated clutter.

5.4

5.4

Friendly Fire 2008

director
Andreas Kaiser
Here, a snorkel lens, much
like an inverted periscope,
was added to the camera and
allowed the lens into this trench
from *Friendly Fire,* where a bulky
camera body could not get.

Recommended viewing

The camerawork on *Madame Tutli-Putli* is extraordinary, with deliberately erratic movements plotted to echo handheld live-action camerawork. It gives a spontaneous feel to the story, as if the camera is responding to the puppets. Animation moves tend to be smooth, because of the way they are plotted, but the moves in this film are appropriately loose and dynamic. When you are working on your own camera moves remember that they are the same as animation moves in that they need to start with small moves, and any switch in direction needs to read clearly.

5.5

Beneath the Moonlight 2011

director
Enrique Ortega
producer
Gaston Fuenzalida
Animating a character inside this
tram in the Chilean film *Beneath
the Moonligh*t, was made easy
by a removable ceiling.

5.5

Strobing

Strobing is an unhelpful illusion whereby an object or character judders distractingly, or appears to move backwards, even though it has been physically moved forwards. This occurs when there is confusion about the overall direction and shape of the movement. It is common during camera moves when the speed of the move is not consistent, incrementally, with the character's movement, causing the character to shift about within the frame, interrupting the through line of its movement.

A quickly rotating wheel might appear to be standing still or moving backwards due to one spoke of the wheel moving forwards into its predecessor's position exactly, or just behind it. The viewer's eye then wrongly makes the assumption that the spoke has moved the shortest distance and moved backwards or stayed still. Drawn and CG animators can blur the image with speed lines to help avoid this. It's not quite so easy with stop-motion.

Various tricks can help, such as adding trailing items suggesting the direction of movement, or giving each spoke a distinguishing detail or colour – it is essential not only to be aware of how a character has moved through its spatial environment but also how it has moved through the camera framing. Make the direction clear and readable.

Similarly, walking characters are particularly susceptible to jerkiness. It's easy to spend so much effort on getting the feet and leg positions right that you physically knock the torso back in the odd frames without realizing it, whereas the torso should be constantly moving forwards. Any conflicting movement will judder horribly. Spend time checking that every piece of a character is moving in the appropriate direction (plotting this movement on the screen with progressing dots will help).

Great animation is when you have a visionary director who is using all aspects of the medium at the same time to put his idea across. That's a film where the music, the sound effects, the drawings, the backgrounds, the motion are all working together. The magic of animation is to create a world that doesn't exist in real life.... All of the artifice falls away and you're left with the sheer joy of life.
Stephen Worth

Tools and techniques

5.6

I Wish I Went to Ecuador 2011

animators
**David Bunting and the pupils
of Bricknell Primary School**
A still from the extraordinary
and epic film made by Bricknell
Primary School, *I Wish I Went to
Ecuador*. Filmed in Cinerama, the
camera gets right in among the
action. Every pupil in the school
was able to contribute to this
remarkable project, even if it was
just making a tree. The top image
shows a great use of depth. Note
the essential and practical use of
a cushion in the bottom image.
It's fantastic that animators so
young can produce an amazing
film, and a Cinerama film at that.

Single or double frames

One important decision is whether to shoot in single or double frames (ones or twos). Should you have 24–25 different individual frames per second or should you make a movement only every two or three frames? More often than not, the choice to shoot on double frames is a choice made out of economy rather than artistry. It is possible to 'get away' with shooting on doubles, and many animators love it, but it is exactly that: 'getting away with it'.

Watching a piece of doubles animation is harder work and very much less enjoyable than a piece of singles, as the viewer's brain has to fill in missing information. We try to create an illusion of movement, but by shooting on doubles we are literally stopping the movement, then starting it again; 'stop-motion' in the worst sense. It can never be smooth, but the staccato effect can sometimes be appropriate.

Financial needs and schedules usually necessitate shooting on doubles, and it's often the default setting on introductory stop-motion apps. With a first film you may not have a choice, but be aware that it can restrict the lushness and detail of the animation. With just 12 frames per second you are unlikely to be able to do much softening at the ends of moves, or subtle quivers of a lip, or a delicate tremble of the hand. Doubles do give a certain raw energy that might be right for a scene, but if you are trying to get a lyrical quality, the more frames the better. With 25 frames per second you can put in much more detail and information, leading to more sophisticated and rounded animation that flows as credibly as possible. Of course, there are some actions for which even 25 frames per second aren't enough;

such as a woodpecker in action. Drawn and CG animators would definitely smudge the animation here. With stop-motion, we'd probably move the head back and forth through a greater extreme in single frames, and help show the effect of the pecking through a secondary action such as wobbling tree trunks and falling leaves. Again, it is not about being literal but making it read.

Before you start filming, try animating the same piece of action, in singles and then in doubles, for the same length. The different results will tell you which way to go.

It is sometimes the technique you are using that dictates whether to shoot on singles or doubles. Sculpting a clay figure 25 times per second is not just labour-intensive; it also doubles the amount of unwanted movement and 'boiling' on the surface. Similarly, your puppet may have an armature that can't actually cope with the finesse of fine movements, and so bigger double frame movements have to be the answer. There is also nothing to stop you mixing singles and doubles in the same action. You could start a heavy object moving with a series of tiny single frame increments, and then once the object is up and moving you can switch to double frames, but, honestly, you will notice the difference. You'll notice the difference too, if you shoot a close-up in doubles although you can get away with it more easily in long shots. Many animators are reluctant to shoot anything in double frames because they want to make everything flow (though this is not the same as making everything balletic and lyrical). With a double frame you are immediately putting a destructive break in this flow. However, double frames can be effective to suggest an inordinately slow movement.

At the heart of this debate is the size of the increments between frames in proportion to the size of the frame. If the increments cover a tiny amount of the frame, and link to the previous image, you'll have smooth animation. If the increment covers a large amount of the frame, the animation will fall to pieces, as it stops relating to the previous image. For this reason, the big move you do in wide shot simply won't work in close-up as there's just not enough information to help the viewer link the two frames and see it as smooth movement. The best approach is to analyse the sort of movement you want from your characters, and the capabilities of your puppets. If you have the option, try to learn to shoot in singles and make your choice after that to suit your style and budget.

Be aware that doubles on a huge cinema screen are cruelly exposed, where the reality of the increments could translate into a matter of feet, and the animation looks anaemic. Watching the same animation on a small mobile device, where the difference between the increments is barely discernible, it will read well. So it's important to know who is going to watch your film, and where? But please don't be pressured into shooting on doubles; make that choice yourself.

5.7

5.7

Foxed! 2013

directors
**James E. D. Stewart and
Nev Bezaire**
This 2013 short film, *Foxed!*,
makes effective use of 3D.

Movement and pacing

If you can't manage real camera moves, most films are made with high-definition digital, and the quality is so good that this allows some basic camera moves to be added in post-production. However, be cautious with these shots as they can easily appear obvious and flat, especially when these post-production movements are seen alongside physical camera moves. This is because the post-production move will be more of a zoom than a real change of spatial perspective.

The more use you can make of the depth of a real set, the more effective the camera moves will be. Imagine a puppet standing alone in a white space with no detail. A camera move would be redundant as there would be little to suggest any changing perspective. But if you add foreground pieces and long corridors trailing away, the slightest camera move will read effectively. Many recent features have been shot in 3D, making the most of the natural spatial depth of the sets and camera moves. The shooting process is complex, requiring extra preparation and acute precision, but it is becoming more and more accessible, and it would seem an appropriate development for stop-motion, although some audiences are resistant to wearing glasses and the drop in luminosity and clarity. Time will tell if this is the way forward. Certainly there are even phones that show films in 3D effect without the need for glasses.

Camera moves help the rhythm and pacing of a film tremendously, although they can be very difficult to achieve in stop-motion. The famous model-train sequence in the Wallace and Gromit film *The Wrong Trousers* (1993) is a great example of pacing. This sequence has been helped by ingenious blurred backgrounds (both painted as blurred wallpaper and moved during the exposure), giving the impression of speed.

However, if your story is dependent on fast and complicated camera moves, stop-motion may not be the way to go. Remember, a CG and drawn camera can go absolutely anywhere, but a stop-motion camera not only has to be animated each frame, its access is also limited by its physical presence and everything that goes with it. This can be overcome by clever set building, sympathetic budgets and schedules, but it is an element that directly affects the narrative.

In the theatre, while you recognized that you were looking at a house, it was a house in quotation marks. On screen, the quotation marks tend to be blotted out by the camera.
Arthur Miller

5.8

Sleight of Hand: A Story in Stop-motion 2012

director
Michael Cusack
Director Michael Cusack on the set of *Sleight of Hand*, alongside the paraphernalia needed for a camera move.

A major problem with lights on a stop-motion set is that they are usually left on all day, and the slightest flicker, or movement in the lamp, or a bulb blowing, can ruin a shot. Any change of colour intensity or brightness will immediately register between frames. As with the sets, the lighting rig has to take into account the access requirements of the camera and animators, and particularly the need for bulbs to be changed. Do check too that no one can fall over the stands, or that nothing will wobble them. Suspend your lamps if possible.

Lighting can affect a film in many ways, but its main purpose is to let the audience see what the directors want them to see. However, with stop-motion, lighting can also help with the movement and with the spatiality of the sets. There's little point in having highly sculpted and textured puppets if a barrage of front and fill lighting is going to flatten everything. The lighting should show off every contour of the puppets and the depth of the sets. Likewise, the movement of the puppets will be emphasized if there are shadows or dappled lighting (through the use of gobos) for them to move through. To achieve this you should work closely with the lighting crew to plot the movement of any characters in a scene.

Remember that texture and detail can be enormously effective in adding credibility to a film, but they are easily lost if these are hidden in shadow. Usually, however standard the lighting, you will need adjustments for each set-up, so do check the continuity if you are shooting out of sequence. Lighting cameramen are very prone to use white foam bounce boards to give faces some fill – inevitably these find their way right in front of an animator, who will be fighting for his space.

5.9

Work together! Happily, digital cameras and smartphones don't need so much light as film, and this can make a set cooler and more comfortable. Remember, we are working with miniature sets, and the lighting can be as rich in detail as the sets and costumes.

5.9

Iluzia 2012

directors
Udi Asoulin and Uriah Naeh
Two stills from *Iluzia* where CG and stop-motion look to exist in the same world, thanks to some beautifully delicate and radiant lighting.

5.10

5.10

Mother's Song 2012

director
Linda McCarthy
A warmly lit still from Linda McCarthy's *Mother's Song*, using depth and shadows, all helping to make the most of the textures of the set.

5.11

5.11

The Owl House 2008

animator
Jessica Cope
The harsh reality of a set transformed into something living and credible, through all the elements of lighting, animation and detailed set dressing.

5.12

Shadows

Like pauses in movement, shadows are
an equally important part of lighting, giving
drama and suspense, and a real sense of
geography. As most stop-motion takes place
on table tops, with the lighting high above,
it's all too easy to give the impression that
none of our sets have ceilings. But, with a
little planning, lighting can give the suggestion
of an architecture that has not been built, or
trees that aren't there, or a time of day, or
warmth or cold. They can also help suggest
a mood, much like colours.

Depending on the conscious artificiality
of your plot, don't be frightened of using
lighting as part of the storytelling, dimming
or **crossfading** at the end of scenes, or
highlighting areas in pools of light. Give each
scene a particular look with the lighting.
The artifice of animation lets it respond well to
this theatricality. Lighting is not just functional.

5.12

Tchaikovsky – An Elegy 2011

director
Barry JC Purves
A still from *Tchaikovsky –
An Elegy* happily embracing
artifice with every element.
Photograph by Justin Noe.

Tools and techniques

5.13

5.13

The Gravedigger's Tale 2013

director
Min Young Oh
A beautiful example of set design, colours, composition, puppets, costume and lighting all coming together.

Crossfading is the technique of fading out one image or sound while simultaneously fading in a second image or sound. This can apply to lighting.

As with lighting, sound is too often treated as an afterthought, but it is a vital element of any film. As such it should be considered at the beginning of the pre-production process along with all the other storytelling elements. As the stop-motion process doesn't allow us to record any live sound when filming, everything has to be created from scratch, and it can be tempting to illustrate every step and every rustle of cloth.

You might be armed with a whole library of effects during the sound dubbing process, but these usually get slowly cut for being too heavy handed or for simply cluttering up the visuals. The secret, as with everything animated, is in being selective, and only using sound that helps the story or the atmosphere. Most cartoons use sound effects to highlight the comedy and energy in the squash and stretch movements with a barrage of swanee or slide whistles and whooshes, but somehow the physicality of puppets doesn't always lend itself to such exaggeration.

Of course, this all depends on the tone of your film, and the extent to which your storytelling relies on sound. Consider whether adding the sound of a character skidding to a halt with a screech fits the action perfectly, or adds some extra energy to the character that wasn't there in the acting, or whether it is too much. Would the inevitable laugh be appropriate?

A careful sound mix can help suggest the spatiality of the sets, and it is essential to have the voices balanced according to the geography of the characters. In an extreme wide shot you are unlikely to hear the characters as clearly as in a close-up; likewise, you don't want a character at full volume in a close-up, and in the vocal recording the performers must be aware of this spatiality.

Ambient sound is useful in complementing the set and lighting design. As with all these elements, try not to always think of sound as a literal reproduction of real life; sometimes the most unlikely objects can provide the most appropriate sound to a particular visual. Most studios have libraries of effects, but it's satisfying to create live effects for the finished picture. The timing works so much better when they are created specifically for the animation. Remember that silence can also be very effective.

Dialogue is not always present in animation, and this gives you more license to play with the storytelling aspect of sound. Remember, in every frame we shoot, we are trying to make a small puppet seem credible as a larger figure. Sound can help give the puppet weight, attitude and character, just as much as the animation.

5.14

5.14

Lo Guarracino 2004

animator
Michelangelo Fornaro
Based on a Neapolitan tongue-twisting song from the 18th century, Michelangelo Fornaro's gorgeous short *Lo Guarracino* mixes human actors and stop-motion with tremendous wit. The artful combination of the song, stylized design and cabaret style give an artifice that lets the animation feel comfortable alongside the live action – with the stop-motion shot against a green screen and inserted into the live-action footage.

Music

Music can often seem a more natural partner to animation than dialogue. Animation is about movement with emphatic use of rhythm, climaxes, surges and moments of calm, as is music. When music and animation work together they bring out qualities in the other, complementing each other. The sublime artificiality of music seems to augment the artificiality of animation. For this reason, music should always be discussed at the start of planning a film, but you do need to think what it is there for.

You can use music simply as a background, to set the scene or help suggest the emotion. However, it can be so much more satisfying when it is used as part of the storytelling itself, with the music being conspicuously upfront as with a ballet. In this way, music can help push the animation away from a comfortable reality into something more interesting and exciting. If any scene requires a degree of choreography, then you should ensure that you have access to the music ahead of filming. Do familiarize yourself with the nuances and structure of the music well before you begin animating. I would suggest that even the most basic ability to read music will be helpful; at least being able to recognize the visual patterns in the structure of the music score.

5.15

5.15

Jason and the Argonauts
1963

animator
Ray Harryhausen
This skeleton battle is one of
the most perfect sequences
in all stop-motion. Bernard
Herrmann's appropriately
percussive and rhythmic score
celebrates the quirkiness of stop-
motion while making it a thrilling
action sequence. Every element
in this sequence works together
to produce something no other
technique could have managed.

Beats

We've seen how stop-motion needs to flow from one frame to another, from one shot to another; music can help this enormously, giving a shape and discipline to what can be a fragmented process. Experience will show you whether hitting the beat comes from the surge of a movement, or the strong pose itself. In live action, actors and dancers can show the beat in a variety of subtle ways, but I suggest we need to be more emphatic, holding the pose on the beat a frame or two longer. Anything to do with beats will need planning as you will constantly be thinking ahead, making sure your animation will get there for the next beat. The music for my film *Next* drove the film forward, and was precisely worked out in terms of structure ahead of the filming; the beats giving me the guide to how many poses I needed to tell the story. I could have animated without the musical shape, but I suspect I would have wandered from the strict rhythm.

Try to incorporate any music you are using in the animatic. You will get a more accurate feel for the rhythm and shape of the film. It's generally easier to choreograph animation to music, than it is to write music for animation filmed without music.

There are so many ways of using music in your storytelling. One extreme is to have a full orchestra announce every action as in the glorious *Tom and Jerry* films, or you can use it more subtly as in Michaël Dudok de Wit's film *The Monk and the Fish* (1994) where the music sets the tone and delicately echoes the structures of the film. Not only are the two worlds (the monastery and the world outside) different through design, colour, pacing and movement, but the music is distinctly contrasted with different instruments, complexities and rhythms for each world. Many animators enjoy working with the discipline that music enforces, though it does not allow for improvisation or inspiration on the set (it is not usually possible to lengthen a piece of music to fit the action and so the action has to fit the music). Don't forget that you will generally need permission to use someone else's music in your film.

For the film *Tchaikovsky – An Elegy*, I learnt the piano pieces, and whilst there was no actual keyboard, the movements were accurate if a little more emphatic. A line drawn on the monitor helps effectively register the fingers. As with most aspects of animating, it helped to think ahead, anticipating where the fingers would be in a few frames' time.

5.16

5.16

Tchaikovsky – An Elegy 2011

director
Barry JC Purves
Tchaikovsky playing his
imaginary piano.

Highly artificial art forms, such as opera, lay out their communication conventions with no apologies. Simply, they sing instead of speak. Even so, it sometimes jars to have an opera singer speaking naturalistic dialogue after a wildly elaborate aria, as the conflict between the two conventions is exposed and awkward. Similarly, animation is often set within fantastic worlds with strange perspectives and odd environments and peopled with gloriously bizarre characters. Naturalistic dialogue can sit uncomfortably in these settings, and it would be a shame to hamper extravagant creations with mundane dialogue. It's important that the dialogue enjoys the same stylistic freedom as the other elements of your film.

First, of course, you need to work out just how important the dialogue is in your film, and how much plot and character information it is revealing. Many animators are more comfortable using artificial forms of dialogue such as singing or rhyme or even voice-overs. It's also worth remembering that most emotions can be conveyed through detailed body language, and this is certainly more animation friendly than a wealth of dialogue with minimal movement.

Most dialogue requires close-ups and cutting back and forth between characters in a conversation; this definitely limits the movement potential of the characters and the film itself (although it is much simpler to film than more action-led scenes). The characters will need some form of mouth movement, which may be too technical, too fiddly, or time-consuming for your budget. Too often, when not used well, dialogue can be a didactic and lazy way of telling what is happening rather than showing it.

Lip-synch

With dialogue comes the tricky issue of lip-synch, and many animators can get sidetracked with the pursuit of precise movement. Naturally, if the characters are speaking it will look odd if there is no movement of the mouth at all – the dialogue could be wrongly interpreted as narration. A lack of mouth movements can also make it difficult for the audience to easily understand who is speaking, unless the body language is clear. Of course, if the body language is completely clear then you may need to ask yourself if speech is necessary.

If you do choose to have dialogue, do ask yourself just how naturalistic you need it to be. If the styling of the puppet means you are unable to produce all the complex mouth shapes speech needs, then it's often wiser to loosely suggest the lip-synch (a simple mouth that can open and close in several stages is often effective if you concentrate on the rhythm). To be absolutely accurate, speech needs teeth, a tongue and a very pliable pair of lips, but most puppets simply don't have that detail, especially when the characters are animals who do not initially possess the mechanics for speech. Animating the intricate movements of a tongue inside a mouth is physically awkward and much easier for CG artists.

5.17

5.17

Una Furtiva Lagrima 2012

director
Carlo Vogele
A real fish lip-synching to Caruso
in Carlo Vogele's *Una Furtiva
Lagrima* with surprising accuracy.

Tip: Avoiding lip-synch

There's no getting away from the fact that
lip-synch slows the shooting process down
with stop-motion, and also adds to the
budget. Most children's programmes use
dialogue and subsequently sufficiently detailed
mouth movements. These programmes
are then sold abroad, with the characters
re-voiced, making a mockery of the original
lip-synch. A crafty solution to this problem
is to invent an expressive but universal
language – the ever mischievous penguin
Pingu has his own lexicon of understandable
sounds. Regardless of the language being
used, try a certain amount of stylization in the
lip-synch, concentrating more on the rhythm
and the arc of the phrase and breathing. Be
careful too, that overly fussy lip-synch does
not draw the attention from the more directly
communicative eyes.

5.18

5.18

Coraline 2009

director
Henry Selick
For *Coraline* and *ParaNorman*
the Laika team developed an
elaborate use of replacements,
rather than internal mechanics,
for some stunningly precise
and lively lip-synch, with a
surprising amount of nuance.
The necessary resources to
produce this effect are out of
reach for most animators, but
the results are astonishing.

5.19

**Gilbert & Sullivan –
The Very Models** 1998

director
Barry JC Purves
Mr Sullivan in full song. Though
he had no tongue and no teeth,
following the strong rhythm
of the music and versatile
mouth shapes with regular
breaths made for convincing
lip-synch. Photograph by Jean-
Marc Ferriere.

Tools and techniques

Vocal performances

However you use dialogue, it is essential that it is recorded and broken down into frames on the **bar sheets** long before filming. An animator can fit loose mouth shapes to the dialogue much more easily than an actor can fit his or her voice to already filmed animation.

When recording the voices for stop-motion, try to get as much physicality and spontaneity into the voices as possible, as well as an awareness of the geography of the scene. Most animators will enjoy picking up on all the little breaths and pauses; seeing a puppet apparently stuttering over a word brings it to life. Seeing a puppet anticipate an action or take a breath gives it immediate life. Once again, it is the little unexpected moments of recognition that work so well.

A cold mechanical voice, treated almost as a voice-over, will not sit comfortably with a lively puppet. It is therefore vital to describe to the actor exactly what the puppet will be doing; are they running along a beach shouting or are they whispering in a cupboard?

It helps to have the vocal cast in the same space looking at each other, reacting to each other naturally. If this is not possible, have someone reading the lines off microphone so you don't have an actor performing their lines in isolation. Technically, it's wise to leave a gap between each line of dialogue, but try to avoid the actor anticipating that break.

Pre-recording means that the animation performance has to fit around the vocal performance. This can be inhibiting to the animation, therefore in an ideal world the animator will have some input into the voice work (such as suggesting certain bits of character business or physical actions that will affect the vocal performance). Make sure you listen to the dialogue and music on your work station as you shoot, noting every accent and pause. Refer to it as much as possible, especially anticipating what sounds come next. As with most elements of animation, it is essential to think a few frames ahead.

Bar sheets or x sheets/dope sheets. These sheets contain the dialogue or music broken down into accurately timed sounds spanning numerous frames, helping the animator choreograph the action or mouth shapes. This is essentially a visualization of the sound, showing the rhythms and silences. It is our equivalent of a musical score. Most animation software can now show the audio track as a sound wave on the screen, though this is more about timing than mouth shapes.

Shooting with digital technology has opened up almost unlimited possibilities for special effects. However, many stop-motion animators still prefer to do as many effects as possible on set. This direct approach certainly gives the effects an integrity within the image, which the mixture of CG and a real set doesn't always manage. Low-budget CG can sit unhappily and flatly in a very spatial world, so try to make sure any CG elements, such as thrown balls or other objects, are rendered in the same lighting conditions and cause shadows, and are in or out of focus as necessary.

It is enormously satisfying to create effects in the same space as the characters. This may be something of a Luddite view when technology can create such astonishing imagery, but it harks back to the origins of stop-motion with its simple tricks accomplished with nothing more than smoke and mirrors. There is also a naïve perception about the ease of CG imagery, which undermines the skill and ingenuity of the artists involved. This assumption that an effect is simple and somehow less impressive because a computer has been involved is entirely erroneous. However, many stop-motion animators still love getting their hands dirty. If you do, you'll probably be happy coming up with creative ideas on set.

The way that you use special effects will probably depend on the sophistication of your film, but try to use imagination before immediately resorting to technology. It's more satisfying if you can control things on the set. However, if you do embrace CG for certain effects, make sure this is all done in the storyboarding stage. We can't get away from doing enough planning.

Tools and techniques

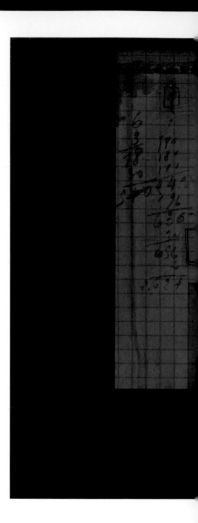

5.20

5.20

A Life Well-Seasoned 2012

director
Daniel Rieley
A Life Well-Seasoned is a
beautifully textured film using
low-tech paper characters and
sets with some backgrounds
generated in AfterEffects. It was
directed and written by Daniel
Rieley from Arts University
College Bournemouth, UK.

5.21

5.21

Corpse Bride 2005

directors
Tim Burton and Mike Johnson
Tim Allen animating the
characters from *Corpse Bride* in
a complex scene with a gloriously
detailed set; these kinds of
scenes are usually only feasible in
big-budget feature films.

Pickups are additional shots filmed after a sequence has been completed, due
to some continuity error or a plot detail that requires more clarity.

Editors on stop-motion films have a hard job, as it is simply not practical to shoot enough extra footage to allow the luxury of trying different cut points or the rearrangement of shots or even alternative takes. We can only shoot what is deemed necessary. Occasionally, on a big set piece scene, it might make sense to have extra cameras shooting secondary detail. However, this can be difficult as there are often tricks (such as supports being hidden from the camera by the puppets' bodies) that would be exposed with a second camera. So the importance of getting the film right in the animatic is essential. I could be glib and say that the editing happens in the storyboarding and animatic, but it never quite works like that. It takes precise judgement to decide whether the time allowed for by a drawing in the animatic is enough to convey the necessary plot on the set, and what happens on the shoot can be somewhat unpredictable.

Spontaneity should be encouraged within the strict parameters of the shots, but it can make continuity difficult, especially if a film has been shot out of sequence. The unpredictability of stop-motion makes it difficult for action to naturally flow into a previously filmed shot. If two shots don't match, the editor will need to disguise the lack of continuity by cutting away to an extra unplanned shot, which can then interrupt the intended flow. Practically, it helps if these changes are noticed by the director on the studio floor. Usually, by the time the editor is at work assembling the sequence, sets have been cleared away, or the scene has moved on, and it's not possible to go back for a **pickup**.

All this has been made substantially easier with shooting on digital. Now, shots can be enlarged, or the framing shifted a little, or characters may have been shot against a green screen to allow them to be used again against a different background. A hold on an action can be extended or shortened if the timing wasn't quite right. Depending upon the economics of the film, a library of stock shots can be built up – this is certainly not ideal, but it is practical. But don't begin to see the digital process as some sort of safety net.

The animator can help give the editor flexibility by always shooting a few extra frames, even if it means overlapping some action. It's so easy for an animator, absorbed in the filming, to see the shot as a complete entity and bring things neatly to a halt – but the editor's job is to make every shot flow into the next smoothly. If two sequential shots have several frames of overlapping action, it will help the editor choose the exact moment to cut, for general pacing or for better synchronizing with the dialogue or music.

It will always help the editor, too, if the animator gives a good reason for a shot to be cut. Cutting to a close-up suggests something of interest is about to happen – it's even better if that something has already started to happen, motivating the cut. Cutting on a move will always help the action flow.

Tip: Leading into the next shot

It helps to lead a new movement
through a cut by giving enough
frames of the incoming action.
One or two frames of a new
movement are not enough as it will
just look like a twitch at the end of
the shot. There needs to be enough
movement, possibly six frames, to let
it register as a movement. It may feel
awkward while shooting this on the
set, and look odd when you watch
the shot back, but when the action is
carried on into the next shot the cut
will be smooth and invisible.

5.22

Paint on glass

animator
Caroline Leaf
Some techniques, such as
painting on glass, let the images
transform from close-up to long
shot, without the need for actual
cuts, producing a very lyrical and
continuous form of editing. It's
not much fun if you have to start
again though, as the physical
artwork will inevitably have
evolved or been destroyed.

Flowing from shot to shot

Editing must have seemed a strange and disorientating concept to the first audiences, especially jumping from one location to another in consecutive frames, or from wide shot to close-up. This is not how the human eye works at all, so it is important that the images flow without too much disorientation. Just as the animation of each frame must relate to the frame before and after in order to flow, so sequential shots and cuts should be fluid. Cutting from a wide shot with a character prominently on the right of frame to a close-up of the same figure on the left of frame will jar with the viewer. But if the figure is on the right in the wide shot and in the close-up shot, then the transition is less awkward for the eye. It flows. This needs particular care with the wider aspect ratios.

It isn't just the staging that needs to flow. The speed of a movement needs to match from one shot to another, which can be hard when shots have been filmed days apart and by different animators. The change from shooting in singles to doubles in subsequent shots can jar too. Equally, if you cut from a brightly lit shot against a red background, to the same character shown from a different angle with a blue, shadowy background, then your scene just won't flow, unless, of course, you deliberately want to create a disconnected feeling. Do remember, though, that animation struggles to flow at the best of times, so the more help we can give it using all the elements of film-making, the better. And this is where an editor can pull a film together.

Editors are removed from the blood, sweat and tears of the filming process and so are not precious about cutting or restructuring sequences – anything to make the storytelling work. Stop-motion shots tend to be shorter than with other forms of animation and film-making, because of many factors, such as running out of time, fatigue, a puppet falling over, the set wobbling or a light blowing. All these can abort a shot, making it hard to sustain a lengthy shot. These difficulties are an inevitable consequence of the physical nature of stop-motion, and new, necessary shots that save a sequence must be allowed for; however, long sustained shots are an exciting challenge and have a sense of achievement about them. Free of physical demands, CG can more easily accomplish sustained shots, such as the epic market chase sequence in Spielberg's *The Adventures of Tintin* (2011), but the planning necessary for this single shot still takes the breath away.

Every cut causes a beat, and so it is important to be aware of any changes to the rhythm of a sequence that an unpredicted shot could cause. A film should move like music, with slow sequences intercut with quicker sequences, with troughs and peaks, tensions and releases. The pace isn't just dependent on the action of the story; it is also dependent on the rhythm caused by alternating different-sized shots, and lengths of shot, or changes of colour and sound. Remember that a shot of just four frames of blurred CG action can still be read by the viewer, but a four-frame shot of stop-motion would be much harder to read. The more different a shot is from its predecessor, the longer it will take to read with the viewer.

All of these elements affect the rhythm. Too much spontaneity on the studio floor and this essential rhythm might get lost. Editors can stand back and see the whole picture better than most.

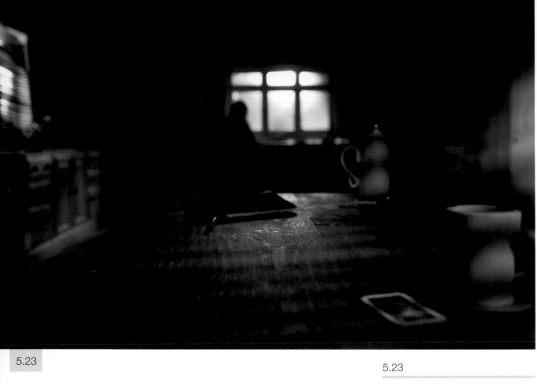

5.23

5.23

Tomorrow 2010

animator
Bob Lee
This still uses bold lighting,
effective set and prop design,
dynamic composition and good
use of focus – all the elements
working together to produce a
very atmospheric frame.

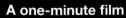

Filming

So you've got your story, your characters and your puppets... but are you ready to start filming? Here are a few points you might want to consider before you get started:

- Have you made the set as comfortable as possible, with everything to hand?

- Do you have the props you need?

- Can you see the monitor easily?

- Do your storyboard and barsheets have enough information? Frame the shots so there is enough room for the action but close enough to see any necessary detail. Think through the shot before you start animating and structure your day.

- What story do you need to tell in each shot?

- Find an order in shooting each frame. Relate every frame to the previous and to the next, checking every limb is going in the right direction.

- Animate with an awareness of where the camera is.

- Give the puppets a breath as they start. Allow time for every gesture to read. Do not rush things.

- Perform the puppets with rhythm, clarity and strong poses.

- Try to shoot a little extra overlap to each shot as this will help in the editing.

- Try and document everything, ticking off each frame as you go. Keep playing back the shot, but remember that a frame is only part of a bigger phrase.

In the next chapter, we'll finish by editing your film...

6.1

In this final chapter we will not only look at how to get clear readable animation but also how to make it mean something. We'll talk about the particular qualities and quirks of stop-motion, its unpredictability and its physicality, and how to make sure that every frame counts. We'll try to encourage inventive, imaginative animation, rather than straightforward literal animation. We'll look at how to give the illusion of elements such as weight and inertia, which help produce credible animation, and we'll stress the important aspects of performance, timing, and acting – essential to any movement. Finally, we will look at how shooting digitally has liberated animation.

6.1

A Midsummer Night's Dream
1959

director
Jiří Trnka
This beautiful film contains some outstanding performances. It was originally released without dialogue, telling the story through music, pantomime and dance. Later an English-language version was released, narrated by Richard Burton. Trnka's multilayered film *The Hand* (1965) also features a wonderful reversal of the

And so, with all the pre-production completed, you're ready to animate. This is the fun part, and this is really why we work in stop-motion. Remember that though the animation will seldom match the images in your head, with enough preparation and patience, they could be even better.

Hopefully on your set you will have at least a lighting cameraman, and someone, maybe the director, or studio director, necessarily structuring your day. This will leave you to concentrate on the animation. How much you are expected to shoot every day is always down to budgets and the standard of animation required. Feature films often shoot a walk through and a final rehearsal, and then expect perhaps two to three seconds per day. This luxury is made necessary by the high standard of animation required for a feature film, with the animation having to stand the scrutiny of large cinema screens. For television series work a daily rate can be between eight and 12 seconds. This is fast and doesn't allow for any rehearsal or retakes, which can be exciting.

It's also hard, physical work, but you can make it easier by being fully prepared, comfortable, and knowing exactly what you are doing when you start a shot. It's unlikely that you'll shoot every shot on a film, and even less likely that you'll shoot in sequence. It is therefore essential that you have a storyboard near you to check exactly how your shot fits in with the larger scheme of things and with the continuity of neighbouring shots. Also, check the puppet before each shot, testing that the tension of the joints will allow for easy movement.

If necessary, stand in a quiet spot and act out the scene, just so you can internally feel the choreography of the action. Do not feel embarrassed, as this will help you immeasurably. We are performers after all. Using a mirror to watch yourself perform the scene can be useful, but remember that it can be confusing if your puppet bears little resemblance to you. Most films will have the dialogue recorded before filming begins, so listen to this several times before you start. Try to catch the rhythm, breathing and accents of the actors. Animating little vocal tics, such as breaths or stutters, ties the voice closely to the puppet, and pleasantly surprises an audience.

In a crowd scene it's tempting to have two animators working on the shot, but the communication necessary between the animators can slow the process down, and you may get several very different styles in one shot; you may also just get in each other's way. Most animators are happier by themselves, however much concentration it might require. This leads to a more satisfactory continuity of performance within the shot. If you can animate a whole sequence, then that's even better.

Movement and performance

Get comfortable

It is vital to make yourself comfortable at your set. Check that you can reach everywhere the puppet will walk, and that you can reach underneath the set for the magnets or tie downs. Make sure that the camera and even the lights and reflecting boards won't get in the way of your access. Develop an awareness of where the camera is. It is important to ensure that there is sufficient space to rest your elbows on a solid part of the set; this will give your hands good solid leverage. Without this resting place your arms are much more likely to wobble. Also, ask yourself whether you have all the props or the replacements you need. How about tools? You will obviously need a monitor, a recording device, a soundtrack, the bar sheets and the storyboards. Other more easily forgotten tools include sticky gum, toothpicks and sharpened lollipop sticks (for reaching areas that fingers can't), allen keys for tightening joints, pens for making marks on the monitor, maybe a surface gauge, tweezers, a ruler to plan the space and the steps taken by the puppet, sculpting tools, masking tape and so on.

It will seem like a lot of clutter, but all of these tools will come in handy. Do also ensure that you can reach everything comfortably, and position the monitor within your eye line when you are animating. Being forced to turn away from the set to look at the monitor is likely to disorientate you each frame. Avoid this in order to maintain some sort of muscle or spatial memory of the scene. Your time on the set will also be made easier if you can avoid treading over cables each frame, so clear the floor of any hazards – hazards to yourself or that could jeopardize anything happening on set. Consider whether the set is too cold or too warm and make what adjustments you can. If the floor seems hard or cold, do put some carpet or a soft rubber mat down.

Tip: Be prepared

Walk through the action in your head, making discreet marks to aim for or even pin figure drawings on the bar sheets for poses you need to hit on certain cues. Having some sort of bar sheet, with the timing of the dialogue or music all clearly broken down into frames, is great discipline. Check that the camera framing is wide enough to contain all the planned action.

Get ready

Stop-motion requires animators to spend long days on their feet, bending and stretching under the heat of the lights, and often in cramped conditions. These physical quirks are a serious consideration, especially when most other forms of animation let you sit in a comfortable chair for most of the day. For us, there's usually some backache along the way, and eye strain from focusing on objects so closely in bright lighting.

The shooting units are usually surrounded by black drapes, not just for lighting but also to help create a space where it is easy to focus. To add to this effect make sure that you put away anything that might break your concentration, as concentration is an essential part of the process. In other words... turn that phone off! These details may seem trivial, especially to drawn or computer animators (or film theorists), but they are a vital part of the stop-motion process.

This is outside of your control, but it is worth noting the importance of having flexible hands and fingers. Large chunky hands may not allow much fiddling about with tiny mechanics, so make sure that your puppet suits your ability to manipulate it.

Above all, before you click that first frame, be absolutely certain that you know exactly what the shot is about. Getting four hours into a shot and then discovering that your character is not holding a vital prop could be disastrous, and it is your responsibility to avoid this.

6.2

Out on the Tiles 2010

director
Anna Pearson
The set from Anna Pearson's *Out on the Tiles* showing that even a simple set-up soon gets busy. You can see the holes in the floor left by using tie downs. Magnets are an alternative technique but difficult if the character has high heels.

6.3

Chiodo Brothers set

An animator in action on a Chiodo Brothers set, with the monitor conveniently in his eyeline.

Movement and performance

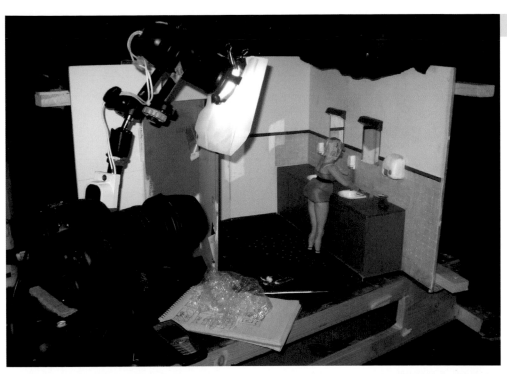

Get started

Hold the puppet with one hand so that the main body is rock solid, and you are able to move the 'animatable' part with the other hand without affecting the rest of the body. This does take practice. It's essential that you use both hands in the process, as a casual one-hand technique will see the puppet wobbling. This is a constant challenge in stop-motion; everything needs to be solid and yet free to move.

When physically animating, judge an increment first by how the puppet feels in your hand, then see how that has translated to the screen. The screen is ultimately what counts, however be wary of concentrating on the screen rather than the puppet. As you move your puppet, try and find something in your field of vision to measure the move against, whether it is a detail in the background, or a shadow on the floor, or a mark on the monitor or your own fingers. It helps to have a visual, real or mental, record of how much you have moved so you can increase or decrease or replicate as necessary – a graphic and muscle memory are huge bonuses for stop-motion. Having the digital record is great, but having a mental record is even better.

Most actions start with a thought or a reaction – these can be best signalled by having the puppet take a breath or blink; all showing the beginnings of a thought process.

Some animators watch the whole sequence after every frame taken to see how the movement builds up. Others prefer only to check the previous frame to see that the movements all relate – feeling the main movement through the puppet, and then refining or gently correcting it by looking at the last frame. Do what feels right for you, but ensure that you do not become disconnected from the puppet. This relationship is what stop-motion, and anything to do with puppets, is all about.

Checking the previous frame is also useful to see whether any lights have blown, or any props fallen over, or whether you have moved the camera. Most recording devices have an 'onion skin' option that allows you to see a transparent image of the previous frame superimposed on your current frame. This is perfect for directly comparing frames, and for seeing the increments. A physical mechanical gauge placed on the set with a pointer indicating a position on the character can help you judge a subsequent increment, as can drawing on the monitor screen. Many programs allow you to leave a trail as you go through the shot, or to plot a path in advance. Good concentration and focus will help, and try to keep to a routine of checking the various elements of the animation in sequence – the lights, the camera move, the set and so on.

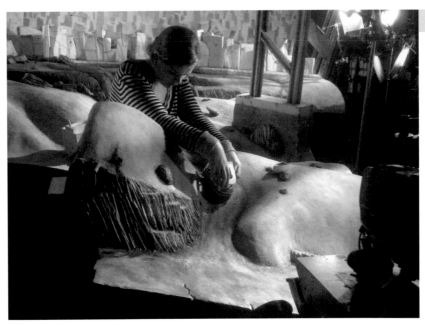

6.4

6.4

Sunday Drive 2009

director
José Miguel Ribeiro
Here, animator Marike Verbiest
reaches in to animate on the
set of José Miguel Ribeiro's
Sunday Drive. Access for the
animators often has to be
cleverly disguised.

We saw in Chapter 3 how the anatomy of your puppet will affect the way it moves. Big feet will lead to a comedy walk with the knees having to be lifted high to flick the feet through. Conversely, if your puppet has short legs it will have a tiny, fussy stride. With other forms of animation it is sometimes acceptable to cheat by allowing for a movement that defies the anatomy. Drawn characters, particularly, can stretch and squash as necessary. With puppets, and again this is part of their appeal, you are dealing with tangible limbs. Some characters can be given replacement limbs when they are needed for particular shots, but this can break the integrity of the puppet's physicality. Using, overcoming, and playing with this physicality is part of stop-motion's appeal.

The extent to which one can stretch a solid character depends on the material and on the tone of the film. Plasticine allows a certain amount of flexibility, but the audience might not accept Aardman's Wallace or Gromit elongating as they run around a corner, as Tom and Jerry do. Whatever your puppet's limitations, the conventions of the character's moves have to be set up immediately in a film, and only broken after very careful thought.

Lively movement

Animation needn't necessarily move with the smoothness of ballet, or reflect real life, as long as the audience can read the intention behind every frame of the movement. Jerky animation can work well if it comes across as deliberate. Good animation is about controlling and guiding the movement so that the significance, the emotion and the storytelling are understood with absolute clarity.

The technique and mechanics of stop-motion filming cannot ever reproduce an exact copy of live movement. A puppet will always have its own distinct way of moving. Whether this is attractive or not is another matter, but it's not something we should apologize for. Instead, we should revel in its quirkiness.

Much live-action movement is too subtle, too complex, too fussy and too erratic to be replicated in just 25 unblurred frames per second of animation. In live action, characters can move during the exposed frame; the resulting blurring gives the eye sufficient information about the direction of movement. With stop-motion, although complicated rigs can move a puppet during exposure, our characters are usually static in each frame, which makes a huge and crucial difference.

Stop-motion is about giving the idea of movement, the illusion of it, through being selective. However sophisticated the armature on your puppet, you simply will not be able to reproduce all the movements, all the strange little tics that happen in live action. It would be foolish to try. A puppet has limitations; it has a mechanical skeleton, which usually has far fewer joints than its human or animal equivalent, and it must contend with the force of gravity.

Movement and performance

These 'limitations' will be a drawback only if you are trying to reproduce reality, but they should really be liberating. In stop-motion, we have the freedom to produce movement that borders on dance, as we are expressing so much through our characters' body language. Stop-motion can still be subtle, but we have to enjoy the artificiality of the movement, and relish it. It's a waste to reproduce what live action does when puppets can be more florid or more mannered or more characterful or simply more static.

6.5

6.5

Mary and Max 2009

animator
Adam Elliot
A heartbreaking still from *Mary and Max*, Adam Elliot's feature film revels in the lo-tech, hands-on qualities of stop-motion.

On *Mary and Max* the rule was that there would be no straight lines, no perfect circles, everything had to be a bit flawed because the script is about flawed characters.
Adam Elliot

Dynamics

It is vital to give the audience as much information as possible about the movement, height and weight of the character, as well as how it reacts to the environment and why it is doing what it is doing. Finding elements that lag behind the main action, such as a trailing hand, can have the same effect as a blurred frame as it tells the viewer which direction things are moving. It's also important to balance strong, open and excessive movements with moments of calm and stillness – stillness is an essential part of movement. This variation of dynamics gives so much life to characters.

If a character is suddenly stopped by hitting a brick wall (in reality a harmless balsa wood or plaster construction), you can imply the solidity of the brick wall, or the character's momentum, by the way in which the character bounces back with a judder. Conversely, if it's a soft wall, you can imply the energy being cushioned by the wall. Without suggesting these real-world dynamics your character may simply look like a puppet in a set.

Enjoying movement

To enjoy stop-motion it helps to enjoy movement. Animation is a very physical medium and studying activities such as dance, animals in action, sculpture, mime, and sport, where the body is expressive and often in extreme poses, can help animators enormously. Try to think like a dancer who, stuck with a very rigid anatomy, attempts to amaze the audience by seemingly crossing the line of what is physically possible. Animators, with puppets, are much the same. A puppet's movement is much more impressive when it flirts with its limits; but if it blatantly crosses those limits, defying gravity anatomy or logic, then it becomes very much less credible.

Many techniques from the world of dance can be used in stop-motion, as long as they are properly adapted. Dancers often 'pop' or 'snap' into a strong pose to accent it. This energetic flick is hard to translate directly into stop-motion as it would simply take too many frames, and it could easily look like an awkward jolt. However, it is possible to play with changes of rhythm that give the same effect. In dance, this movement works by suddenly stopping and seemingly ignoring the physical rules of inertia. With stop-motion, it is almost the opposite. A puppet's movement works when the audience sees it affected by gravity, weight and inertia, as long as the effects are expressed clearly and deliberately.

Experienced dancers have the ability, after suitable rehearsal, to dance through muscle memory, without having to consciously think through the moves. It flows naturally with one move leading to the next, directed by the music. While you won't always have the luxury of rehearsals, it should be possible to manage something similar by being very familiar with the storyboards, except your role is both that of a dancer and choreographer. I wouldn't recommend starting a move without having thought out how it will play through the shot.

Dancers do exactly what we do; they tell stories and reveal characters and thoughts through movement. Watching, and if possible taking part in, dance is invaluable in learning the potential and limitations of the human body. It is so helpful to be truly conscious of what your body is doing, how the weight is shifting, how it is balanced, and the shapes and through lines you are making. This awareness will help you 'see' movement, as it is not always easy to sketch stop-motion movements beforehand.

If your schedule or budget allows for a walk-through, checking the potential positioning and the lighting, grab it. It certainly helps if you can visualize the shapes and movements of the characters ahead of actually animating them, whether you have acted them out physically or internally.

Let it read

One of the most important lessons of stop-motion is that every gesture should 'read'. This really is the most significant advice I can give. You can ensure this happens through the clarity of the pose and by ensuring you include enough meaningful frames to tell the story and show the mechanics. In live action an object or character might change direction in the exposure of a single frame. To achieve the same effect in stop-motion we need to spell it out for the viewer. We must show the object slowing down, the change of direction, and then speeding up again. Really show the effect of inertia on the object, angling it as it changes direction. If something is going to be done, make sure it is done clearly. Likewise, if something is not moving, let it sit there without twitching, and give the viewer time to realize it is sitting there deliberately. One frame does not make a pause.

Musical metaphors

Strong poses are an essential part of animation, just as they are vital for dance and sculpture. However, the length of time you keep a puppet in such a pose is a fine balance. Don't waste a lovely shape by only letting the viewer see it for a single frame; ease into it, hold it, and ease out of it. If you hold a pose for a long time, a puppet can still be communicating even through not moving. The trick is not to let the puppet suddenly die, with everything stopping on exactly the same frame. Some gentle secondary movement flowing and overlapping through the pause will keep the puppet alive. As silence is an integral part of music, so stillness is a part of movement; with music we hear a note fade naturally, and so movement comes to a halt naturally. To suddenly completely stop a movement would be like a bad edit in music.

Just as single notes in music mean very little until they are put next to another note, until they are placed in some sort of structure and rhythm, so it is with individual frames and gestures. They only make sense as part of a bigger phrase. It is very helpful to think beyond the actual frame you are animating. Imagine how it fits within a larger arc of the movement. If you think of movement as no more than a series of individual frames somehow magically put together to produce some greater movement, it just won't work.

You need to see the architecture of the whole gesture and action. This is all about making movements flow into each other, by relating each frame to the previous one, and having in your head the much larger shape. A frame is only the single key on the piano, or using another appropriate metaphor, that of writing, a single letter. A full stop very clearly indicates the end of a thought or statement, or gesture, but a comma will link two thoughts or ideas into a single arc. Get away from the idea of thinking about individual frames, and think about the scene and story as a whole.

A very good trick to help the flow and the overall shape of a move is to imagine a marker on any given point of a puppet: the end of a finger, or the chest, or knee joint. Mark each frame on the monitor as you move through a shot and if the line traced is clear, with a smooth defined shape, whether it be a constant forward line or a series of gentle curves, you can guarantee that it will be good animation. If the line is zigzagging erratically, the animation will be much less effective.

6.6

The right angle

dancer

David P. France

In the first shot (above left) the camera just misses the strength of the pose from this particular angle, though there are still some interesting shapes. In the second shot (above) the legs have clarity, but the arms don't read quite as well. In the third still (left) every element of the body reads perfectly for the camera. As with animators, a dancer has to make sure that his body shapes are seen by the audience from the best angle.

6.6

How much potential for movement is there in your film? In stop-motion, movement is not just confined to the way a character moves. The way in which an environment reacts to a puppet can also often help to suggest movement. As a character rushes through the frame, a disturbance of leaves or debris on the floor, or banging doors, can all help the illusion. Long scarves and bits of costumes trailing behind the character create the idea of movement.

A movement is also more noticeable if there is background detail to move against. A puppet of a colour similar to its bland background, moving through flat, shadowless lighting, will not be as effective as a puppet standing out from its background moving through shadows. Movement in a sideways plane obviously registers more strongly than a movement towards the camera, but that sideways movement doesn't make the most of the real space that is one of the great advantages stop-motion has over other forms of animation. Placing objects in the foreground, so that characters can move behind them, creates huge depth. Similarly, the choice of lenses can help accentuate a movement and depth. Close-up lenses tend to squash and flatten the space while wide-angle lenses make a small space look bigger, with any movement towards the camera having more dynamics, making the depth of the space more noticeable.

Speed

Every movement can benefit from a change of speed. It is important to understand that fast movement comes from widely spaced increments, and slower movements from narrowly spaced increments. An accelerating movement will have gradually increasing increments. It might help you to visualize this by drawing a movement as drawn animators do, seeing how the increments cluster for the slow start of the action and then spread out for the fast bit.

As you are developing your animation try to find the dynamics in every action, the changes of rhythm and accent. This can be hard to coordinate, especially if there are several characters, or parts of characters, all moving at different speeds. You will need to remember and coordinate all the different tempos, just like a conductor or a choreographer. New animators sometimes try to simplify the movement of the various different limbs by creating symmetry in the poses (this is known as 'twinning'). Unless it is used as a conscious part of the storytelling, this can look very lazy and uninteresting. Even though animating two limbs doing different things is harder to coordinate, it is well worth the effort as energetic movements in one hand can be balanced by more measured movements in the other. Any musical training, such as playing the piano, comes in handy here.

6.7

6.7

War Horse 2007–

directors
**Marianne Elliott and
Tom Morris**

In this powerful National Theatre
production, each horse is
beautifully performed by three
very visible operators. This
shares much with stop-motion,
where the audience are complicit
with the technique of bringing the
characters to life, and that is an
essential part of the storytelling.
It is more rewarding than a
literal approach. Much of the
puppeteers' work is giving breath
to the horses.

Being less literal

Sometimes a gesture, such as a subtle 'tut' with a raised eyebrow, will require so many frames to mechanically spell out the action that the timing becomes laboured and the meaning is lost. In this case you need to find other ways to portray the same meaning, such as a slight sigh. Likewise, if your character must push a button, the actual button may not move or it might be too fiddly to manipulate. This will require you to emphasize the action in other ways, such as making more of the wrist pushing the hand, and more of the actual release. A character banging away on a piano keyboard may not have the dexterity in its fingers to accurately spell the notes out, so a more conscious emphasis on the rhythm of the hands would work. None of this is necessarily realistic, but in stop-motion the realistic way is seldom the most appropriate, the most expressive or the most readable.

As animators, everything we do from the narrative to the movement itself is an illusion, and we have to find the clearest, most direct way of creating this illusion. A small puppet representing a full-scale human weighs very little, so to animate it landing after a jump, we need to give the illusion of a much larger and heavier character. This could be done by emphasizing the compression in the knees and body, and letting the arms swing down heavily; by taking a few more frames to spell out the action. This immediately takes the timing away from live action, but it does tell the story clearly. However, as with the 'tut' above, too many frames can make the gesture less effective.

Always ask how fast something should move, and the answer should be dictated not by the size of the physical puppet in front of you but by the imagined weight and scale of the character, its anatomy and its emotion. If the character is meant to be the size of a house it will probably move with smaller, slower increments than something meant to be the size of a small cat. The speed of the character immediately suggests its weight. And emotionally, a melancholy character is unlikely to move as fast as a character delirious with joy. Keep questioning yourself about how and why a character will move. How can you represent the character's emotions through movement? Don't take the easy route of having a character saying that they are happy. Instead, show that they are happy. Children's programmes often finish with all the characters laughing – sometimes the puppets don't have moving mouths and so have to laugh with their whole body in a staccato rhythm. This less literal approach is how you need to start to think. It's far more imaginative and satisfying.

6.8

Monsterous Murders 2013

directors
**Sarah Davison and
Sarah Duffield-Harding**
A character from Sarah Davison
and Sarah Duffield-Harding's
Kickstarter-funded short,
Monsterous Murders.
A single eye and a dramatic
pose are enough to register a
strong presence.

6.9

A**hole Robot 2012

director
Chris Walsh
The idea of the mechanical
having an independent thought
process and life echoes the
very nature of animation. Here,
a robot gets up to dastardly
deeds in Chris Walsh's short
A**hole Robot.

Show the mechanics

Every action is made up of several pieces of action, and it's important that the mechanics of what is happening are seen. Just the action of a character rising from a sitting position has to include a moment when the character makes the decision, the thought process, to rise. This activity in the eyes is the start of the movement and then the head follows. Then the viewer needs to see the weight transferred from the character's bottom to over the feet planted solidly on the ground, which involves the torso leaning forwards and the backside lifting free and balanced backwards. Then the backside has to be pushed under the torso, as the torso straightens up, with the head finally coming to rest on the shoulders. This is the end of the movement. All this happens in a few frames in live action, but it helps to create a credible movement if we linger over the storytelling moments and changes of direction, enjoying the curves inherent in the action.

You don't have to stop at the key moments, but highlighting them by giving that moment a few more frames, lets the action read. Make sure you can find these moments in every action, and see where the movement starts and finishes.

Again, movement is so often like a piece of music. A single sustained note, like a single smooth continuous movement, is dull. But if you start to add rhythms and accents, and different pacing, it will become very much more interesting. Fortunately with stop-motion, it is quite hard to provide a single sustained movement. Human error leads to irregular increments. Computer animators have to learn to remove the precise mathematics from these moves and give these increments rhythm and dynamics. Stop-motion animators have to use the

irregular increments and turn them into something deliberate. Have a look at the joyously quirky movements of the French film comedian, Jacques Tati, in films such as *Mon Oncle* (1958) and *Playtime* (1967), where his walk becomes a masterclass of timing and character tics.

Jumping is a complicated movement in any form of animation; it requires every part of the process to be shown clearly. However, in stop-motion it is a particularly tricky move. There are a variety of ways to achieve it. Stop-motion puppets, by their very nature, make good solid contact with the floor. This is usually an advantage, but sometimes it is hard to make them look light on their feet. Standing on tiptoes takes subtle and strong mechanics in the feet joints and possibly a suspending string, or a rig and good balance. Having puppets go even further and actually jump is even more complicated but well worth the effort.

To animate a run without the puppet leaving the ground can look clunky, but to suspend a puppet takes time and inevitable post-production work, but thankfully shooting on digital continues to make our life easier. Rigs can support characters off the ground, as long as a plate has been taken, allowing the rig to be digitally painted out and replaced by the background. This is tricky and painstaking, but it is part of the process now. It has quite revolutionized the kinetic and athletic capabilities of a puppet, and we've never before seen such acrobatic action as is common now. If you can afford the time, do get your puppets off the floor.

You can also suspend characters on wires or fishing line, which on film could have been lit to be pretty invisible, but the sharpness of digital will expose the wires. Get in the habit of taking an empty image of the beginning and end of a shot to help patch any corrections needed in post-production. A camera move complicates this, as you may need to film the camera move without characters so you have all the background detail from every angle, and for this you'd need a computer-controlled rig.

6.10

Toby's Travelling Circus 2012–

director
Barry JC Purves
producers
Richard Randolph and Chris Bowden
Toby's Travelling Circus – Li and Ling on the high wire. Having puppets walking on a high wire is made easier, though not easy, through rigs that are removed digitally in post-production. Photograph by Dick Dando.

There is nothing mystical about performance. At its most basic, it is about letting every controlled movement, every angle of the head, every change of rhythm, every pause, every walk, every raised finger and every blink express and reveal, with clarity, something about the character or the narrative. It is about presentation to an audience or camera. It is about using the blink of an eye, not just to serve as a biological function but to show a moment of punctuation in a thought process.

All of this takes a thorough understanding of body language. And do be aware that body language is not always universal. Many gestures come from specific cultural references, or learned and coded roots, while others are pure logical mime or a physical expression of some psychological behaviour. A single raised finger has many widely different interpretations around the world, from being a literal point through being a polite acknowledgement, to a gross insult. It is therefore important to use open and honest forms of gestures and body language; movements and shapes that, though not literal, are completely clear in their meaning and emotion. Once you find exactly the movements that can define characteristics such as anger or yearning, you can apply that just as well to a household object as to a fully articulated puppet; there may be several defining movements, but try to combine them into one clear, precise, and preferably, understated movement. The less clutter the better.

In any language, the order of the units of vocabulary and the ways in which they are combined are of prime importance, as are the inflections and rhythms. Body language is no exception; it needs punctuation and grammar to separate or complement each gesture. Rather than words you will be working with a whole complex lexicon of gestures, poses, attitudes and airs. The different combinations can produce unlimited meanings. Give each character his or her own clearly defined repertoire of gestures, which is not dissimilar to the leitmotifs Wagner used to signal recurring characters and themes in his operas. Be careful, though, not to play that single, defining expression in every frame. Characters are rarely that simple.

6.11

Plume 2011

director
Barry JC Purves
The disturbing 'shadows' from *Plume*. Removing detail from eyes unsettlingly deprives most thought processes. Photographs by Justin Noe. A Dark Prince production.

6.11

Casting

In much the same way that actors are cast in particular roles; animators are often cast for particular qualities. Some animators are equally at home in all types of scenarios, but you'll find that some are much better at slapstick, while some are better at the quieter character-driven scenes. A good director will recognize this and give animators appropriate scenes. It will certainly serve you to practise as many different emotions and styles as possible. Stop-motion not only demands that you become an actor, it also asks that you play a wider range of characters than any actor would. In addition to human characters, you will be asked to perform monsters, inanimate objects, fantasy characters, totally abstract ideas and characters that don't have any recognizable means of communicating human emotions.

However, at the heart of most animation will be a clear human characteristic – in the world of animation even vegetables, cute animals and monsters have emotions and desires and frustrations and goals. There has to be a motivation, even behind the actions of an all-munching dinosaur. What is it defending? Why is it there? Your huge challenge is to make such things seem credible and natural, and tell stories that the viewer will identify with. You need to give these inanimate objects goals, frustrations and resolutions. You need to be able to see the metaphor and fable in every situation and character.

Timing

When you have been animating in the studio for several hours on an action that may only be a couple of seconds of screen time, it is all too easy to think that the filmed action feels longer. Try always to think in terms of the timing in the world on screen, and not in the studio; and don't confuse the two. It is surprisingly difficult to separate these two time scales, but it does get easier with experience. Similarly, never try to do an important scene at the end of the day when you are tired – the puppet will unavoidably look tired too.

New animators find it particularly hard to give a held action, or pause, enough time to register. Instead, they often rush on to the next action, killing the moment and ruining the pose. To avoid this, you just need to give the audience sufficient time to see the physical mechanics of a movement or, again, the thought process and reactions involved in a piece of acting. Spell it out. Let it read.

When you are animating the reactions of a character to a loud bang it's tempting to have the character jump back the very next frame, but that would deny the thought process and ruin the credibility. If you wait a few frames and see the face register before the body reacts, there's more of a credible story. Don't be frightened of explaining a movement in too great a detail for your audience. One clear gesture, which has time to breathe, is better than several that are rushed. Timing is no mystery; it is just about showing the thought process and the mechanics.

Walking

As mentioned in Chapter 3, your puppet should combine practicality with interesting design, and have sufficiently long and accessible legs to allow the character to walk if necessary. Ideally, you need to hold the torso rigidly with one hand, while manipulating the legs with the other. This is where a third hand would be ideal. It's essential to make sure that the torso is moving forward in each frame as it can easily get knocked about. It's worth tracing the progress of the torso, and every limb, by marking it off on the screen, making sure the increments are going in the right direction. But, as with most actions, it's important to understand what defines the motion. The inverted V of a walk, as the back foot peels off the floor and the front foot slaps down, is the strongest shape in a walk and needs to be emphasized. Don't rush through this moment. The poses of the back leg flicking through tell less of a story than the key pose. Give the viewer time to see that pose. Don't just divide the walk into equal increments; see the change of pace as the foot is put down. Look at the rhythm of a person walking; it's all too easy to get overcomplicated and lose this.

In live action, the subtleties of a walk are immense, but you are unlikely to have the puppet, the patience, or the time to accurately copy these, and nor should you. Once again, it's about selection and animating only what is essential and what defines the action. A march uses sharp, rigid limbs with very little softening at the end of moves, whereas a walk will see the relaxed arms and trailing hands following through with a slight delay. As is so often the case with stop-motion, when making your puppet walk, you should aim to make it credible rather than realistic.

Exercise: Reconstruction

Take a few seconds of an iconic live-action scene from a film, and reconstruct it with very basic household objects, analysing exactly what it is about the performance, the movement, the composition and the drama that make it work. Hone it down to just the key moments, such as a certain tilt of the head or a tentative step or the well-timed look over the shoulder. Go directly to the heart of the scene. An animator should be able to look at any movement and find the storytelling part of it.

Animal movement

Four-legged creatures are always a challenge, not just for the sheer complexity of working out the choreography of each leg, and their different stages of locomotion, but also for trying to get access to each of the legs. A four-legged character is much more 'closed' than a character on two legs and this certainly complicates the animation process. Likewise, there's double the amount of securing to the set than with a biped.

Therefore, if you have animal characters in your film you must decide very early on how they will move and communicate. If you choose to keep an animal character on all fours, you are losing a certain amount of expression in the limbs, which will be needed for locomotion. This means you'll need to convey all the expression through the head and tail, assuming your animal has one (tails and ears are a vital part of communication in animal characters). Alternatively, if you put them on two legs, you lose a certain amount of natural animal behaviour but gain much recognizable human behaviour.

It's interesting to see how, even in the flexible world of animation, some animated animals lend themselves to becoming two-legged versions and some clearly don't. Perhaps it is about size. Perhaps it is about freeing the movement from the restraints of realistic behaviour and celebrating movement as a result of expression rather than anatomy. The dancing hippos from Disney's *Fantasia* (1940) come to mind.

Exercise: Anthropomorphism

In stop-motion, animating animal movement is rarely about recreating actual animal movement. Instead, it is more often about creating human movement within the loose parameters of animal anatomy. Anthropomorphism is still a huge part of what every animator faces each day, and animals are an intrinsic part of metaphor and fable.

Choose a friend or relative and try to imagine what animal they most resemble. Ask them to strike an appropriate pose and then find a clear line, shape and story in that pose. It should then be possible to translate the pose into a rough sketch of the appropriate animal. It doesn't need to be beautifully drawn; it just needs to catch the energy and character of the pose in animal form. If you find it easy to translate a human model into, perhaps, a giraffe, then you are certainly an animator. It is what we do, and it's certainly an exciting challenge.

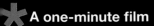

Putting it together

So, we've made it to the final stage and you're ready to finish your film: make sure to consider the following:

● Edit the film so that it races to the conclusion with variations of pace.

● Keep checking that the story is absolutely clear and every plot point and thought process has time to read.

● Add appropriate sound effects and music and special effects, but do not smother the story. Work out whether the music is for background or is part of the action.

● Find a friend to look at it with fresh eyes. Don't be precious about cutting what does not work.

The need for patience is brought up every time stop-motion is mentioned, and it is true that stop-motion animators need patience. That doesn't just mean being calm. It means unreservedly accepting that the process is laborious, tedious, ridiculously fussy, stupidly slow and will require a huge amount of effort to produce a relatively small amount. Accepting this can be challenging, and many people who begin working in stop-motion ultimately fall by the wayside, finding easier ways to make films. For those of us for whom stop-motion really is part of our lives that is just the nature of the craft. I frequently have retrospectives now of my films at festivals, and it is dispiriting to see my career flash by in a few hours. Is that it? Seeing these small-budget films, they do seem flawed rehearsals for the as yet unmade larger films, and I do wonder if the humble little films can match the huge aspirations I have. Is stop-motion, especially short films, capable of such grand ambition? Yes, I do believe it is, and the flaws make it special and spontaneous and a craft.

However, if you still want to pursue stop-motion and find pleasure in the minutiae of the craft, and shiver with excitement at the resonances of a puppet seemingly moving by itself; then you may soon be hooked. If you can appreciate that the few seconds of film produced in a day is an achievement, then welcome to stop-motion. You will find huge satisfaction in the sheer painstaking fiddliness of the craft, from getting your hands dirty, from trying to control the smallest detail, and even from the sheer repetition of the process. If a small character with beads for eyes stares at you and that look haunts you, and if you want to bring extraordinary and very credible characters to life through the intimate contact of your hands, and if you want these characters, your alter egos, to tell your story, then stop-motion is certainly for you.

You'll need an acceptance that the unpredictable will happen. See this as a positive quality, and don't see it as your film changing but as your film growing. Once you accept this, stop-motion really can be addictive, as you have made something seemingly move by itself; in effect, created some life – and a life that will go on untouched by time and age. People who have never tried it can sometimes find this need to give things life, this compulsion to tell stories, hard to comprehend, and perhaps that is what gives it a special appeal. Maybe we do feel a bit of an exclusive smugness and pride after a rather exciting piece of animation, when what is obviously a piece of cloth and metal has credibly acted out some scenario or emotion and made someone laugh or cry – and we've done it with just our hands. Such pride in creating has been part of us for centuries.

Stop-motion certainly does require a particular way of looking at things. Not everyone is capable of looking at an inanimate object and seeing a character or an inherently dramatic situation. Not everyone can look at a simple object and ask 'what if?'. The rewards are just as particular, but it is something that you have to love doing, otherwise something very special can seem a lot of sound and fury signifying nothing.

More than 35 years on, I still love every frame. I'm sure you will too.

Plume 2011

photographer
Stéphane Piera
The author pondering the first
sightings of the *Plume* puppet.
The relationship between puppet
and animator is quite unique,
with both supplying equal parts
of the performance.

1896 Georges Méliès develops many of the tricks still used in stop-motion, especially substitution by stopping the camera.

1899 Arthur Melbourne-Cooper animates matches for *Matches: An Appeal*. This was the first commercial to use stop-motion.

1900 In *The Enchanted Drawing*, J. Stuart Blackton mixed drawn animation and objects.

1907 Edwin S. Porter brings dolls and teddies to life in *The 'Teddy' Bears*.

1910 *The Battle of the Stag Beetles* was the first of Władysław Starewicz's stop-motion films to produce detailed performances from insect and animal characters.

1915 Willis H. O'Brien makes *The Dinosaur and the Missing Link: A Prehistoric Tragedy*, just a year after Winsor McCay's *Gertie the Dinosaur* first appears.

1923 Buster Keaton's *Three Ages* features a short animated sequence with Keaton on a dinosaur.

1925 *The Lost World* sees Willis H. O'Brien's dinosaurs appearing on screen with real actors.

1926 Lotte Reiniger's *The Adventures of Prince Achmed* used delicate and complex cut-out silhouettes.

1930 Starewicz makes the feature *The Story of the Fox*, one of the few early animations to follow a darkly comic storyline.

1933 *King Kong* is released, with astonishing animation by Willis H. O'Brien.

1935 *The New Gulliver*, directed by Aleksandr Ptushko, features a live actor and 3,000 animated puppets.

1942 The George Pal film *Tulips Shall Grow* features dozens of goose-stepping characters animated through replacement puppets.

1949 Jiří Trnka makes the feature-length *The Emperor's Nightingale* (also known as *Císařův slavík*).

1952 Norman McLaren films *Neighbours* through pixilation, animating humans as if puppets.

1953 Ray Harryhausen supplies the effects for his first major feature film, *The Beast from 20,000 Fathoms*.

1954 Michael Myerberg and John Paul retell the story of *Hansel and Gretel*, based on the opera by Engelbert Humperdinck.

1955 Gumby, a clay animation character created by Art Clokey, is introduced on US television.

1958 George Pal's *Tom Thumb* mixes animated puppets with actors.

1959 Jiří Trnka makes a spectacular puppet version of *A Midsummer Night's Dream* (also known as *Sen noci svatojánské*).

1963 *Jason and the Argonauts* is released with the classic skeleton battle sequence, animated by Ray Harryhausen.

1965 Jiří Trnka's political film *The Hand* is released.

1970 *Dougal and the Blue Cat* (or *Pollux et le chat bleu*), a feature film, is released, based on the TV series *The Magic Roundabout* by Serge Danot.

1974 Britain falls in love with *Bagpuss*, a children's television show by Peter Firmin and Oliver Postgate, who also gave the world *The Clangers*, *Noggin the Nog* and *Pogles Wood*.

1975 Ivo Caprino animates the hugely popular *The Pinchcliffe Grand Prix*.

1975 Industrial Light & Magic is formed, producing extraordinary special effects for features, with Phil Tippett being responsible for stop-motion in such films as *The Empire Strikes Back* (1980).

1976 Caroline Leaf animates coloured oil on glass for *The Street*, followed the year after by Kafka's *Metamorphosis of Mr Samsa* animated in sand.

1977 *Morph*, created by Dave Sproxton and Peter Lord of Aardman Animations, makes his first appearance on British television. Co Hoedeman wins an Oscar for his short film *The Sand Castle* (*Le château de sable*).

1979 Yuriy Norshteyn makes *Tale of Tales*, which is often cited as the greatest animation short.

Early 1980s Video playbacks appear in studios, enabling animators to see the previous frame, and a sequence as it is filmed.

1981 *Clash of the Titans* was released; this was the last major film for which Ray Harryhausen contributed animated characters.

1982 Jan Švankmajer makes *Dimensions of Dialogue* (*Moznosti dialogu*) and Tim Burton makes his short film *Vincent*.

1983 British animation studio Cosgrove Hall adapt Kenneth Grahame's *The Wind in the Willows*. They will produce many iconic stop-motion TV series, including *Postman Pat*.

1985–6 Will Vinton's studios make the clay animation feature *Mark Twain*, as well as creatures in *Return to Oz*.

1986 The Brothers Quay make their short film *Street of Crocodiles*.

1988 Jan Švankmajer makes *Alice* (*Něco z Alenky*), featuring both live action and stop-motion.

1989 Nick Park's short films *A Grand Day Out* with Wallace and Gromit and *Creature Comforts* are both released by Aardman Animations.

1992 *Shakespeare: The Animated Tales*, was a series of condensed animated adaptations of Shakespeare's plays produced by a multinational collaboration, followed in 1995 by *Operavox*, six animated operas.

1992 Mackinnon & Saunders is formed in Manchester, creating stop-motion puppets for TV, features and commercials. Their first production is Barry Purves' *Rigoletto*.

1993 Tim Burton produces the stop-motion feature *The Nightmare Before Christmas*, directed by Henry Selick. Dave Borthwick directs the pixilated *The Secret Adventures of Tom Thumb*.

2000 Aardman releases its first feature film, *Chicken Run*, directed by Nick Park and Peter Lord.

2003 Adam Elliot wins the Oscar with his clay animation film *Harvie Krumpet*.

2005 Tim Burton's *Corpse Bride* and *The Curse of the Were-Rabbit*, directed by Nick Park and Steve Box, are both released.

2007 Frédéric Guillaume and Samuel Guillaume release *Max & Co*, a stop-motion feature film.

2008 Tatia Rosenthal's feature film *$9.99* is released.

2009 *Coraline*, directed by Henry Selick, is released in 3D. Other stop-motion features released include Adam Elliot's *Mary and Max* and Wes Anderson's *Fantastic Mr. Fox*.

2010 *O Apóstolo* directed by Fernando Cortizo is released.

2011 A French feature film, directed by Giles Penso, *Ray Harryhausen: Special Effects Titan*, is released.

2012 Tim Burton's *Frankenweenie*, Chris Butler and Sam Fell's *ParaNorman* and Aardman's *The Pirates! In an Adventure with Scientists!* are all released.

2013 Ray Harryhausen dies. Brazil's first stop-motion feature film, *Minhocas*, is released.

Page numbers in italics denote illustrations.

A

Aardman, 31, *45*, 84, 120. *See also Wallace and Gromit*
Abyss, The (1989), 41
Achilles (1996), 23
Adventures of Baron Munchausen, The (1988), 38
Adventures of Tintin, The (2011), 185
Alice (Něco z Alenky) (1988), *64, 65*
Alice in Wonderland (Carroll), 65
All My Relations (1990), *94, 95*
allegory, 68, 78
Allen, David W., 42
Allen, Tim, *182*
ambient sound, 170
Anderson, Wes, 44
Animal Farm (1954), *69*
Animal Farm (Orwell), 68
animals
    in early animation, 17
    in fantasy, fable, and allegory, 68
    fur, 26, 86–87
    movement, 212
    in political metaphors, 71
    puppet anatomy, 97, 103, 115
animatics, 135, 174, 183
animators
    casting, 32, 210
    characteristics, 16, 141, 154, 214
    personality transfer, 32
    physical demands, 192
    relationship to puppets, 35, 61, *215*
    skills, 118
    visible, *33*
Ansems, Bianca, *112, 113*
anthropomorphism, 212
apps, animation, 92, 132, 156
Aristotle, 58
armatures
    for clay puppets, 118, 120
    design considerations, 94, 96, 144
    kits, *96*
    single- *vs.* double-frame shooting, 162
art, 50–51, 57
artifice
    in art, 50–51
    in dialogue, 176
    in Greek drama, 58

honesty and truth in, 50–51, 58, 72–73
    in music, 172, 176
    in set design, *168*
    in theatre, *60*
artist–art relationship, 56, 57, *83*, *106, 189*
Asoulin, Udi, *166*
aspect ratios, 140, 185
A**hole Robot (2012), *205*
audience, 62
automata, 61

B

background, 22, 164, 202
Bagpuss (TV series), 46
Balance (1989), *74, 75*
Bambi (1942), 78
bar sheets, 179, 191
Bardin, Garri, 30
*batteries not included (1987), 41
Bear with Me (2008), *124*
beats, 174, 185
Beaver, The (2011), 52
Beaver Creek (2008), *119*
Being Bradford Dillman (2011), *125*
believability. *See* credibility
Beneath the Moonlight (2011), *158, 159*
Bewitched Matches (1913), 17
Bezaire, Nev, *163*
Billy Twinkle: Requiem for a Golden Boy (2012), *33*
Blackton, J. Stuart, 17
blinking, 31, 194
blue-screen technique, 143
blurring, 160, 162, 185
Bobby Yeah (2011), *26, 27*
body language
    character revealed by, 100, 204, 208
    cultural references, 208
    facial expression and, 105
    freedom of movement, 197
    puppet design and, 101, *102*
    vs. dialogue, 176
body shapes, *201*
Bottle (2010), 123
Bowden, Chris, *134, 135, 207*
Box, Steve, 30
Brave (2012), 87
breath, 94, *178,* 179, 194, *203*
Bricknell Primary School, *161*
Britain (2011), 46
Brothers Quay, 70
budget considerations
    crowds, 81

expression, 105
fur and hair, *86,* 87
lip-synching, 177
mechanics, 82
number of characters, 82
puppets, 80, 107
set, *182*
shooting schedule, 190
shooting techniques, 82, 88, 101
single- *vs.* double-frame shooting, 162
storyboards and pre-visualizations, 134
technical and practical factors, 84, *85*
Bunting, David, *161*
Burch, Emma, *125*
Burgess, Darren, *117*
Burkett, Ronnie, *33*
Burton, Richard, *189*
Burton, Tim, 65, 66, 95, *182*
Bush, Bexie, 46
Butler, Chris, 67

C

camera moves
    evolution of, 156–57
    live-action effects, 36, 157, 158
    post-production, 164
    rhythm and pacing, 164
    set depth, 164
    snorkel lens, *158*
    strobing, 160
    studio setup, *165*
    suspended puppets, 207, *207*
cameras, 156, 191. *See also* shooting
Cameron, James, *40, 41*
Carpenter, John, *39*
Carroll, Lewis, 65
Cars (2006), 84
casting, 32, 210
CG animation, combined with stop-motion
    appropriateness of, 105
    Goutte d'Or (2013), *139*
    Iluzia (2012), *166*
    It's a Bird (1930), 127
    panoramic shots, 88
    Plume, 85
    stunt work, 38
CG animation, features of
    blurring, 160, 162, 185
    camera moves, 36, 164
    characters' contact with ground, 26
    colour scheme flexibility, 148

detail, 42
facial expression, 105
fur, 26, 87
group dynamics, 34
panoramic shots, 88
for pre-visualizations, 135
rhythm and dynamics, 206
for sets, 138, *139*
special effects, 180
speech, 176
strobing, 160
sustained shots, 185
textures, 26
water sequences, *85*
characters
    body language, 100, 204, 208
    number of, 58, 82
    psychological depth, 17
Chimp Project, The (2001), *18, 19*
Chiodo Brothers, *98, 192, 193*
Chorlton and the Wheelies (TV
    series), 108
Christmas Dream, A (1946), *49*
Chronicles of Narnia (Lewis), 68
Cinderella (1899), 16
cinema, shooting for, 60, 140, 163,
    190
ciphers, 72–73, *73*
Clangers, The (TV series), 46
Clash of the Titans (1981), 42
clay
    animating, *28*
    armatures, 118, 120
    challenges and benefits, 118–19
    costumes, 144
    cultural resonance, 118
    effects, *118*
    energy, 29
    handling considerations, *30,* 31,
        80, 120
    models, *103*
    painting, *28, 121*
    puppets, 31, 115, 118, 120
    single- *vs.* double-frame
        shooting, 162
clay faces, 31
clay painting, *28, 121*
Clokey, Joe, 45
close-up shots
    budget considerations, 82, 88
    dialogue, 176
    editing, 183
    expression, 101, 105, 114
    movement, 202
    paint-on-glass backgrounds, 184
    single- *vs.* double-frame
        shooting, 162, 163

on small puppets, 104
sound mix, 170
clothing. *See* costumes
Cohl, Émile, 17
Cole, Ron, *114, 115*
colour palettes, 148, *149, 150,* 185
Compost Corner (2012), *142, 143*
confounding the norm, 54–55, *55*
Conti, Nina, *74, 75*
Conti, Paolo, *108, 109*
Cook, Randall William, *39,* 42
Cope, Jessica, *167*
Coraline (2009), 44, 66, 112, *178*
Corpse Bride (2005), 66, *91,* 95, *182*
costumes
    clay, 144
    colour choices, 148
    fabric choices, 144, *145, 146,*
        147
    handling considerations, 94, 144
    movement of, 98, *146,* 147
    scale, 147, *149*
    shoes, 147
    weathering, 140, *146*
Coudyzer, Ruphin, *18, 19*
counterbalance, 21
counterpoint, static, 22
crawling, 87, 116
credibility
    costumes, *146, 149*
    effort and fatigue, 94
    lighting and, 166
    motivation, 210
    movement, 22, 198, 204, 206
    sets, 140
    sound mix, 170
    texture, 140, *141*
    timing, 210
    vocal performances, 179
crew, 190
crossfading, 168, *169*
crowds, 81
Cuppa Coffee Studios, *71, 111*
Curse of the Were-Rabbit, The
    (2005), *30,* 116
Cusack, Michael
    Gargoyle (2005), 82
    Sleight of Hand (2012), *33,* 82,
        106, 139, 153, 165
cut-outs, *80,* 124–28, *125, 126,*
    128

D
dance, 198–99
Danforth, Jim, 42
Dark Prince, 85
Davison, Sarah, *140, 141, 205*

Day Shift (2012), *122*
De Swaef, Emma, *12, 13, 99, 144,*
    145
de Wit, Michaël Dudok, 174
Death of Stalinism in Bohemia
    (1991), 71
Deep, The (2010), 122
detail, 27–30, *28, 29, 30,* 166
dialogue, 82, 170, 176–77, *177,*
    178, 190
Diary of Anne Frank, The (Frank), 78
digital shooting. *See also* shooting
    accessibility of, 156
    camera size, 156
    editing, 183
    effect on animating live, 34
    lighting requirements, 166
    post-production camera moves,
        164
    special effects, 180
    suspending puppets, 206–7, *207*
direction, changing, 199
directors, 132, 135, 210
displacement. *See* projection
distancing, 60–61, *71,* 72–73, *73*
Dodd, Peter, *128*
doors, 141
dope sheets, 179
double-frame shooting, 162–63,
    185
drawn animation, 27, 29
dream narratives, *49,* 76, *77*
Dream of a Rarebit Fiend (1906), 17
Dream of Toyland, A (1907), 14
dresses, 147
Duffield-Harding, Sarah, *140, 141,*
    205
Dumbo (1941), 78

E
Earth vs. the Flying Saucers (1956),
    41
economics. *See* budget
    considerations
editing, 183–84, *184,* 185
editors, 183, 185
educational projects, *161*
Electreecity (2008), *140, 141*
Elliot, Adam
    clay puppets, 118
    Harvie Krumpet (2003), 30, *59*
    Mary and Max (2009), 30, 78,
        131, 197
    Wallace and Gromit (series), 31
Elliott, Marianne, *203*
emotions, 204
Empire Strikes Back, The (1980), 41

Enchanted (2007), 66
expression
    animal characters, 212
    body language (*See* body
      language)
    budget factors, 82
    clay faces, 31
    clay puppets, 118
    eyes, 31, 101, 110, *111*
    facial, 101, *104*, 104–5
    hands, 114, 115
eye acting, 110
eyes
    absence of detail, *111*, 112, *208*
    animals, 103
    character appearance, 100
    in close-up shots, 101
    design options, 103, 112, *208,*
      209
    expression, 31, 101, 110, *111*
    preceding movement, 206
    presence, *205*
    realism, 113
    replacements, 107, 112
    thought process, *111*, 206, *208,*
      209

F
fable, 68
fabricators, 117
fabrics
    costumes, 144, *145, 146*, 147
    puppets made from, 62, *86, 87,*
      98, 144, *145*
    scale of prints, 147
    texture, 147
faces, 31, 101, 104, 105
false perspectives, 138
Fantasia (1940), 212
Fantastic Fear of Everything, A
    (2012), 38
Fantastic Mr. Fox (2009), 44, 87, *91*
fantasy
    landscapes, 38, 66
    perspective in, *62–63*, 66
    special effects, 42–43, *43*
    as visual metaphor, 68
Faust (1994), *118, 119*
feathers, 147
feet
    anchoring, 97, 147, *192*
    clay, 118
    moving, 160, 196, 206, 211
    shoes, 147
Fell, Sam, *67*
Finding Nemo (2003), 44, 68, 84
fingers, 115

Firmin, Peter, 46
First Men in the Moon, The, 43
Flushed Away (2006), 84
flying, 84, *85*
'Food of the Gods, The' (Hitchcock),
    38
foregrounds, 143, 202
Fornaro, Michelangelo, *171*
fourth wall, 50
Foxed! (2013), *163*
frame, set boundaries and, 142
frame size, 163, 191
frames, increments between
    character size, 204
    frame size and, 163
    gauging, 194, 211
    irregular, 106, 206, 211
    reading, 18
    single- *vs.* double-frame
      shooting, 162–63
    speed of movement, 202
France, David P., *201*
Frank, Anne, 78
Frankenweenie (2012)
    budget, 80
    design integrity, 44
    hair animation, 87
    puppets, *91*, 116
    set size, 88
Friendly Fire (2008), 103, *132, 158*
Fuenzalida, Gaston, *158, 159*
fur, 26, 86–87, 116, 147

G
Gargoyle (2005), 82
Gilbert & Sullivan – The Very Models
    (1998), *178, 179*
glass, animating shapes on, *124,*
    128
glass, painting on, *184*
'go-motion' technique, 41
Goutte d'Or (2013), *139*
Gratz, Joan C., *28, 121*
Gravedigger's Tale, The (2013), *144,*
    145, 169
Great Cognito, The (1982), 120
Greek drama, 58
green screen techniques, 14, *15,*
    88, 140, *171*
Grey Wolf and Little Red Riding
    Hood (1990), 30
group dynamics, 34

H
hair, 87
Halas and Batchelor, *69*
Hamilton Mattress (2002), 88

Hamlet (1948), *52, 53*
Hamlet (Shakespeare), 52, 72
Hand, The (1965), 71, *189*
hands, animator, 192
hands, puppet, 82, *114*, 114–15
Handspring Puppet Company, *18,*
    19, 61
Harryhausen, Ray, 42, *43, 173*
Harvey (play), 72
Harvie Krumpet (2003), 30, *59*
Haunted Hotel, The (1907), 17
Head Over Heels (2012), *136, 137*
Headcases (TV series), 71
heads, 106–9, *107, 108, 109,* 116
Henderson, Ainslie, 35
Henry V (play), 58
Her Morning Elegance (music
    video), 44
Herrmann, Bernard, *173*
Hinterland (2010), *102*
Hitchcock, Alfred, 38
honesty, 58, 72–73, 75
Hopewell, Chris, *84*
Horne, Andrew II, *68*
Hugo (2011), 16

I
I Am Tom Moody (2012), *35*
I Live in the Woods (2008), 46
I Wish I Went to Ecuador (2011),
    161
Iluzia (2012), *166*
In the Fall of Gravity (2008), *114, 115*
Indiana Jones and the Temple of
    Doom (1984), 38
inertia, *23, 24, 25,* 198, 199
internal thoughts, externalizing,
    52–54, *54, 55. See also*
    projection
It's a Bird (1930), 127

J
Jackson, Peter, 36
James, Daniel, *101, 157*
Jason and the Argonauts (1963),
    42, *43, 173*
Jiminy Cricket, 72
Johnson, Mike, *182*
jumping, 206
Juran, Nathan, *43*

K
Kaiser, Andreas, *103, 132, 158*
Keaton, Buster, 105
Kezelos, Christine, *78, 79*
Kezelos, Christopher, *78, 79, 83,*
    155

King Kong (1933), 17, 36, *37*, 87, 104
King Kong (2005), 36, *37*
Kohler, Adrian, *18, 19*
Komaneko: The Curious Cat (2009), *56, 57*

L
Laika, 66, 178
landscapes, fantasy, 38, 66
latex, 99
Lauenstein, Christoph, *74*
Lauenstein, Wolfgang, *74*
laughter, 204
Lavis, Chris, *113, 149*
Le roman de Renard (The Story of the Fox) (1930), *16, 17*
Leaf, Caroline, 123, *123, 184*
League of Gentlemen's Apocalypse, The (2005), 38
Lee, Bob, *146, 186*
Lego Movie (2014), 44
Lepore, Kirsten, 123
Les Trois Inventeurs (1980), *128*
L'homme à la tête en caoutchouc (The Man with the Rubber Head) (1901), *15*
Life of Pi, The (2012), 87
Life Well-Seasoned, A (2012), *181*
Life's a Zoo (TV series), *68, 71, 111*
lighting, 26, *99, 166,* 166–69, *167.*
    See also shadows
Linder, Max, 105
Linear Dreams (1998), 65
lip synching, 82, 176, *177, 178, 179*
live-action camerawork, 157, 158
live-action filming, combined with stop-motion animation
    challenges, 36, 42
    close-ups, 104
    facial expressions, 104, 105
    fantasy landscapes, 38, 66
    mixed actors, *171*
    music videos, *84*
    special effects, 17, 36, *37,* 41, 180, *181*
    stunt work, 38, *39*
live-action filming *vs.* stop-motion animation
    beats, 174
    change of direction, 199
    close-ups, 105
    movement, 20, 92, 104, 196, 204, 206, 211
    realism, 24
    storytelling devices, 62, 71
Lo Guarracino (2004), *171*

L'Oiseau (2009), *149*
Lord, Peter, *45, 95, 107*
Lost and Found (2012), *28*
Lost World, The (1925), 17

M
machines, futuristic, *40,* 41, *205*
Mackinnon & Saunders, *91, 93*
Madame Tutli-Putli (2007)
    camerawork, 157, 158
    costumes, *149*
    perspective shift, 66
    puppets, *113*
magnets
    for anchoring puppets, 97, *192*
    for doors, 141
    in puppet hands, 115
Maker, The (2011), 57, *83, 155*
Man Who Was Afraid of Falling, The (2011), *24, 25,* 138
Man with the Rubber Head, The (1901), *15*
Marionette (2012), 57
Marquis (1989), *72*
Mary and Max (2009), 30, 44, 78, *131, 197*
Mary Poppins (1964), 72, *73*
Mascot, The (1934), 17
Mask II (2001/2002), *54–55*
Matches: An Appeal (1899), 14
Mather, Vicky, *150*
McCarthy, Linda, *86, 87, 102, 167*
McLaren, Norman, *18, 19*
Melbourne-Cooper, Arthur, 14
Méliès, Georges, 14, *15,* 16–17
Metamorphosis of Mr Samsa, The (1978), 123
metaphor, visual, 68, *69,* 71, *74, 75*
metaphors, musical, 200, 202, 206, 208
Midsummer Night's Dream, A (1959), *189*
Miller, Arthur, 164
Minegishi, Hirokazu, *56*
Minhocas (2013), 44, *108, 109*
Miss Todd (2013), *133*
momentum, *23,* 198
Mon Oncle (1958), 206
Mona Lisa Descending a Staircase (1992), *121*
monitors, 191, *192, 193,* 194, 200
Monk and the Fish, The (1994), 174
Monsterous Murders (2013), *205*
Monsters Inc. (2001), 87
Morgan, Robert, *26, 27*
Morris, Tom, *203*

Mother's Song (2012), *167*
motivation of characters, 210
mouths, 103, *107, 109,* 176, *178*
movement
    anatomy and, 103
    animals, 212
    background and foreground effects, 22, 164, 202
    body language (*See* body language)
    Burton on, 95
    changing direction, 199
    changing speed, 202
    continuous, 20
    contrast, 198
    of costumes, *146,* 147
    counterbalancing, 21
    dance as resource for, 198–99
    editing, 183–84, *185*
    facial expression and, 105, 194, 206
    flying, 84, *85*
    illusion of, 22, 196, 202, 204
    increment sizes (*See* frames, increments between)
    lighting and, 166
    momentum and inertia, *23,* 24, *25,* 198, 199
    musical metaphors for, 200, 202, 206
    pacing, 164
    persistence of vision, 18
    physics, 198, 204
    realism *vs.* quirkiness, 20, 24, *25,* 92, 196–97, 204
    rhythm, 196, 198, 202, 206, 211
    secondary, 162, 200
    static counterpoint, 22
    sustained poses, 200
    symmetrical, *202*
    through shadows, 166, 202
    visible mechanics, 206
    vs. dialogue, 176
    walking, 160, 196, 211
    weight, 204
Mueck, Ron, 54, *54–55*
Muller, Harold L., 127
music, 172, *173,* 174, *175*
musical metaphors, 200, 202, 206, 208
myth, clay-related, 118

N
Naeh, Uriah, *124, 166*
Neubauer, Vera, 123
Newitt, Jeff, *45, 95, 107*

Next (1989)
    music, 174
    physics, *24, 25*
    puppets, *116, 117*
    Shakespearean conventions, *60*
Nightmare Before Christmas, The
    (1993), *62, 63*
$9.99 (2008), 44
Noah's Ark (1908), 14
non-literal representation, 62, *63*
Norshteyn, Yuriy, 124
Nunes, Arthur, *108, 109*

O
O'Brien, Willis H., 17, 36, *37*
Ocelot, Michel, 124, *128*
Oh, Min Young, *144, 145, 169*
Oh Willy... (2012)
    costumes, *144, 145*
    puppets, *12, 13,* 62, 98, *99*
Olivier, Laurence, *52, 53*
One Million Years BC (1966), 42
One Week (1920), 105
'onion skin' feature, 154, 194
Ortega, Enrique, *158, 159*
Orwell, George, 68
Out on the Tiles (2010), *114, 192,*
    193
Owl House, The (2008), *167*
Owl who Married a Goose, The
    (1976), 123, *123*

P
pacing, 164, 185
painting on glass, *184*
Pal, George, 109
panoramic shots
    budget considerations, 82, 88,
        101
    expression in, 101
    movement, 202
    paint-on-glass backgrounds, *184*
    single- *vs.* double-frame
        shooting, 162, 163
    sound mix, 170
ParaNorman (2012)
    budget, 80
    design integrity, 44
    lip-synch, *178*
    perspective shift, 66, *67*
    replacement parts, 107
    set, 88
Park, Nick, *30*
Partington, Simon, *77*
Pas de deux (1968), *18, 19*
patience, 214
pauses, 199

Pearson, Anna, *114, 192, 193*
Peladan, Christophe, *139*
Penso, Gilles, *43*
performance. *See also* shooting
    camera presence, 156
    casting, 32, 210
    continuity, 32–35
    crew, 190
    instinctiveness of, 34, 154
    manipulating puppets (*See*
        movement; puppets,
        manipulating)
    preparation for, 190
    process, 194
    shooting schedule, 190
    studio setup, 191, 192, *193*
    timing, 210
    tools, 191
    vocal, 179
    walking, 211
persistence of vision, 18
personality transfer, 32, *33*
perspective
    Brothers Quay, 70
    false, 138, *139*
    political metaphor, 71
    shift in, *62–63,* 66, *67*
Pes, 46
physicality, 26–31, 92, 196
pickups, 182, 183
Piera, Stéphane, *215*
Pingu, 177
Pinocchio (1940), 68, 72
Piper, The (2013), *101*
Pipkin (2013), *86, 87*
Pirates! In an Adventure with
    Scientists! (2012)
    budget, 80
    design integrity, 44
    puppets, *45, 95,* 107
    set size, 88
    water scenes, 84
pixilation, *150*
Plasticine, *30,* 31, 99, 196
playback systems, 154
Playing Ghost (2011), *112, 113*
Playtime (1967), 206
Plume (2011)
    budget strategies, 82, *85*
    movement, 22
    performance, *208, 209*
    puppet–animator relationship,
        215
Pogles, The (TV series), 46
political themes, 68, *69,* 71
Porter, Edwin S., 17
Postgate, Oliver, 46

preparations
    animatics, 135, 183
    colour palettes, 148–50
    costumes (*See* costumes)
    on-set effects, 180, *181, 182*
    pre-shooting, 190
    pre-visualizations, 135
    producer and director roles, 132
    sets (*See* sets)
    storyboards, *134,* 134–35
pre-recording vocal performances,
    179
pre-visualizations, 134, 135
Priestley, Joanna, *94, 95,* 123
producers, 132
projection
    ciphers, 72–73, *73*
    dreams, 76, *77*
    honesty through, 75
    substantive themes, 78, *79*
props, *153*
proscenium, 60, 61
puppeteers, *18, 19, 33, 203*
Puppetoons, 109
puppetry, similarities to stop-motion,
    203
puppets, designing
    advances, *91*
    anatomy, 103
    anchoring to set, 97
    animals (*See* animals)
    armatures, 94, 96
    body language, 101, *102*
    budget considerations, 80
    chests, 94
    clay (*See* clay)
    colour schemes, 148, *149*
    costumes (*See* costumes)
    cut-outs, 124–28, *125, 126, 128*
    detail, 27
    early animations, *16*
    expression (*See* expression)
    eyes (*See* eyes)
    faces, 31, 101, 104, 105
    feet (*See* feet)
    fur, *86, 87,* 116, 147
    hair, 87
    handling considerations, 94, 106,
        116, 120, 144, 148
    hands, 82, *114,* 114–15
    heads, 106–9, *107, 108, 109,*
        116
    markers, 200
    mouths, 103, *107, 109,* 176,
        178
    process, *98, 103*
    proportions, *100*

replacements (*See* replacement
    pieces)
sand, 123, *123*
simplicity, *80*, 92–93, *94–95,*
    122
size, 94, 104, 116, *117,* 118,
    192
skin, 98–99, *99,* 120
spatial awareness, 102
stunt work, 38, *39*
texture, 26, *28, 99*
weight and inertia, 24, *25*
puppets, manipulating
    design for, 94, 106, 116, 120,
        144, 148
    suspending, *95,* 206–7, *207*
    technique, 94, *95,* 194, *195*
    walking, 211
puppets, storytelling with
    animator–puppet relationship,
        215
    animator's personality, 32, *33*
    appeal of, 92
    in early animation, 17
    projection, 72, 75, 78
Purves, Barry JC
    Achilles (1996), *23*
    Gilbert & Sullivan – The Very
        Models (1998), *178, 179*
    Next, 24, 25, 60, 116, *117*
    Plume (2011), *22, 85, 208, 209,*
        215
    Screen Play (1992), *97*
    Tchaikovsky – An Elegy (2011),
        91, 93, 111, 141, 146, 168,
        175
    Toby's Travelling Circus (TV
        series), *80, 81, 134, 135, 207*

Q

Quest, The (1996), 75
Quinn, Joanna, 29

R

Radiohead, *84*
Randolph, Richard, *134, 135, 207*
rapid prototype printing, 107
Ray Harryhausen: Special Effects
    Titan (2011), *43*
reading
    body shapes, *201*
    change of direction, 199
    defined, 22
    increments between frames, 18
    movement intention, 196
    single- *vs.* double-frame
        shooting, 162

techniques assisting, 21–22
timing, 206, 210
Real Robinson Crusoe, The (2012),
    44
realism, transcending, 20, 24, *25,*
    92, 160, 196–97, 204
Reckart, Timothy, *136, 137*
Red Balloon, The (1956), 66
Reeves, Richard, 65
registration, 106
rehearsals, 190, 199
Reiniger, Lotte, 124, 127
replacement pieces
    challenges and benefits, 106, 108
    for cut-outs, *128*
    eyes, 107, 112
    hands, 115
    limbs, 196
    mouths, *109, 178*
    Pal's use of, 109
    rapid prototype printing, 107
representation, non-literal, 62, *63*
representational storytelling, 62–65,
    63, 64
Return to Oz (1985), 120
rhythm
    camera moves and, 164
    as editing consideration, 185
    in movement, 196, 198, 202,
        206, 211
Rhythm in the Ranks (1941), 109
Ribeiro, José Miguel, *195*
Rick and Steve – The Happiest Gay
    Couple in All the World (TV
    series), 71, 115
Rieley, Daniel, *181*
Rigoletto (1993), 82, 105
rigs, 206, *207*
RoboCop (1987), 41
Roels, Marc James, *12, 13, 99,*
    144, 145
Roof Sex (2001), 46
Roots of the Hidden (2012), *126,*
    127
Royal Ballet, 65
running, 147, 206

S

salt, *124*
sand, animation with, 123, *123*
satire, *68*
scale
    of costume details, 147, *149*
    of sets, 138, 140
Scorsese, Martin, 16
Screen Play (1992), *97*
script development, 134, 137

Selick, Henry, *62, 63, 178*
Selkirk (2012), 44
semiotics, *131,* 132, 133, *169, 186*
Serkis, Andy, *37*
sets
    accessibility, *133,* 136, *142, 143,*
        158, 159, 191, *195*
    anchoring puppets to, 97, 147,
        192
    aspect ratios, 140
    boundaries beyond frame, 142
    budget factors, 88
    camera movement, 156–59,
        158, 159
    character and style of, 142
    comfort, 191
    credibility, 140, 167
    doors, 141, *141*
    false perspective, 138, *139*
    foregrounds, 143
    front, 138
    height, *142,* 143, *143*
    lighting, 166, 168
    puppet size and, 94, 116
    scale, 138, 140
    size of, 88, *182*
    stability, 136
    studio setup, *136, 137,* 138,
        139, 165, 191, *193*
    weathering, 140, *149*
Seurat, Georges, 54
Sevenoaks, Elizabeth Marie, *126,*
    127
7th Voyage of Sinbad, The (1958),
    43
shadows
    accidental, 156, 166
    effects of, 168
    following out of frame, 142
    movement through, 166, 202
    in stop-motion animation, 26
    texture and, 166, *167*
Shaheen, Adam, *68*
Shakespeare, 52, 58, 60, *60,* 72
Shannon, Pamela Wyn, *86, 87*
shoes, 147
shooting
    angles, 138, *139,* 143, 156,
        158, 201
    aspect ratios, 140, 185
    budget considerations, 82, 88
    camera moves (*See* camera
        moves)
    close-up shots (*See* close-up
        shots)
    editing and, 183
    false perspectives, 138, *139*

shooting (*continued*)
  green screen techniques, 14, *15,*
    88, 140, *171*
  hidden supports, 183
  length of shots, 185
  lighting requirements, 26,
    166–69
  panoramic shots (*See* panoramic
    shots)
  post-production camera moves,
    164
  schedule, 190
  set design and, 138
  single *vs.* double frames, 162–63
  special effects, 180
  suspending puppets, *95,* 206–7,
    207
  sustained shots, 185
  technical advances, 34
silicon, 99, 115
Simpsons, The (TV series), 71
single-frame shooting, 162–63,
  185
skin, 98–99, *99,* 120
Sleight of Hand (2012)
  camera moves, *165*
  characters, *33,* 82
  props, *153*
  set, *139*
  themes, 57, *106*
Slumberless (2013), 77
snorkel lens, *158*
sound
  ambient, 170
  beats, 174, 185
  dialogue, 170, 176, 190
  lip-synch, 82, 176, 177, *177,*
    178, 179
  mix, 170
  music, 172, *173,* 174
  selective choices, 170
  universal, 177
  vocal performances, 179
South Park (TV series), 71
South Park: Bigger, Longer & Uncut
  (1999), 44
spatial awareness, 102
special effects
  fantasy, 42–43, *43*
  futuristic machinery, *40,* 41
  in live-action films, 17, 36–37, *37*
  on-set effects, 180, *181, 182*
  stunt work, 38, *39*
speech, 82, 176, *177, 178, 179*
speed of movement, 202, 204
Spitting Image (TV series), 71
Stanley Pickle (2011), *150*

Starewicz, Władysław, *16,* 17
Stevenson, Robert, *73*
Stewart, James E. D., *163*
stop-motion animation
  appeal of (*See* stop-motion
    animation, appeal of)
  with CG animation (*See* CG
    animation, combined with
    stop-motion)
  challenges (*See* stop-motion
    animation, challenges of)
  evolution of, 14–17, *15, 16*
  with live-action filming (*See* live-
    action filming, combined with
    stop-motion)
  related activities, 198, 199, 202
  techniques (*See* performance)
  as theme in animated films,
    56, 57
  vs. CG animation (*See* CG
    animation, features of)
  vs. live-action filming (*See* live-
    action filming *vs.* stop-motion)
stop-motion animation, appeal of
  animating objects, 45
  building sets, 136
  freedom of movement, 197
  group dynamic, 34
  instinctive performance, 34, 154
  linear shooting, 32
  physicality, 26, 34, 92, 196
  process, 214
  representational storytelling, 65
  transcending realism, 24, 160
stop-motion animation, challenges of
  animator strain, 192
  choreography, 137
  crawling, 87, 116
  frame-to-frame flow, 183
  imprecision, 154
  lighting, 168
  movement (*See* movement)
  shooting, 34, 88, 135, 156, 157
  twitching, 94, 141, 144, 184
  water scenes, 84
stories, animated, *64,* 65
*Story of the Fox, The (Le roman de
  Renard)* (1930), *16,* 17
storyboards
  eye acting, 110
  movement and expression, 101
  planning replacements, 106
  process, *134,* 134–35
  purpose of, 134
storytelling
  allegory, 68, 78
  animation technique and, 57

arc, 66
artist–art relationship in, 57
distancing devices, 60–61, *71,*
  72–73, 73
externalizing internal thoughts,
  52
fable, 68
fantasy (*See* fantasy)
Greek drama, 58
metaphor, *65,* 68, *68, 69,* 71,
  74, 75
perspective shift, *62–63,* 66
projection, 72–78, *73, 74, 77, 79*
representational approach,
  62–65, *63, 64*
themes (*See* themes)
Strange Hill High (TV series), 105
Street of Crocodiles (1986), *70*
strobing, 160
studio setup, *136, 137,* 138, *139,*
  165, 191, *193*
stunt work, 38, *39*
*Sunday Afternoon on the Island of
  La Grand Jatte* (Seurat), 54
Sunday Drive (2009), *195*
Švankmajer, Jan
  Alice (1988), *64, 65*
  Death of Stalinism in Bohemia
    (1991), 71
  Faust (1994), *118, 119*
  materials, 119
Szczerbowski, Maciek, *113, 149*

T
Tale of Sir Richard, The (2006), *128*
Tales from the Powder Room
  (2002), *117*
Tati, Jacques, 105, 206
Tchaikovsky – An Elegy (2011)
  budget strategies, 80, 82
  costumes, *146,* 148
  lighting, *168*
  music, 174, *175*
  puppets, *91, 93,* 110, *111*
  set, *141,* 142
  themes, 57
Team America (TV series), 71
teamwork, 34
technique, story and, 57
technology
  animation apps, 92, 132, 156
  CG animation (*See* CG
    animation, features of)
  digital photography (*See* digital
    shooting)
  playback systems, 154
Ted (2012), 52

Terminator, The (1984), *40, 41*
texture
    clay painting, *28*
    costume fabrics, *144–45,* 147
    lighting and, 26, *99,* 166, *167*
    paper cut-outs, *128*
    physicality and, 26, *27*
    set credibility, 140, *141*
themes
    allegory, 68, *69,* 78
    artist–art relationship, *35, 56,* 57,
        83, 106, 189
    dreams, *49,* 76, *77*
    human experience, *74, 75*
    living/dead conflict, *67*
    mature, 78
    political/social, 68, *69,* 71
    satire, *68*
    stop-motion animation, *56,* 57
    thinking machines, *205*
    tragedy, 78
    them/us distancing, 60–61, *71,*
        72–73, 73
There There (2003), *84*
Thing, The (1982), *39*
thought process
    expression through eyes, *111,*
        206, *208, 209*
    preceding movement, 194, 206
    timing, 210
Three Ages (1923), 38
three unities, 58
3D, *37, 163,* 164
tie downs, 97, 147, 191, *192, 193*
timing, 206, 210
Timothy, Ian, *119, 122*
Tippett, Phil, 42

Toby's Travelling Circus (TV series),
    80, 81, 134, 135, 207
Tom and Jerry (TV series), 174
Tomorrow (2010), *146, 186*
tools, studio, 191
Town Called Panic, A (2009), 44
Trnka, Jiří, 71, *189*
True Family Story (2009), *100*
truth
    artifice and, 50–51
    in fantasy, fable, and allegory,
        68
twinning, 202
twitching, 94, 141, 144, 184

U
Una Furtiva Lagrima (2012), *122,*
    177
uncanny valley, 61
Uncle Creepy (2009), *98*
unities, three, 58

V
ventriloquists, 72
Verbiest, Marike, *195*
Vinton, Will, 120
Viv & Mandy in the Big Clean Up
    (2012), *157*
vocal performances, 179
Vogele, Carlo, *122, 177*

W
walking, 160, 196, 211
Wallace, Joseph, *24, 25, 138*
Wallace and Gromit (series)
    budget strategies, 80
    clay character studies, 31

    Curse of the Were-Rabbit, The
        (2005), *30,* 116
    sets, 142
    Wrong Trousers, The (1993), 164
Wall-E (2008), 62, 68
Walsh, Chris, *100, 205*
War Horse (play), 61, *203*
water scenes, 84, *85*
weathering, 140, *149*
weight, 24, *25,* 204
Weta Digital, *37*
Wheel of Life (1996), 123
whip pan, 21
wide shots. *See* panoramic shots
widescreen, shooting for, 140
Wife of Bath (1998), *29*
Winston, Max, 46
wire
    for fingers, 115
    in puppet skeletons, 96
Wood, Westley, *142, 143*
Worms (2013), 44, *108, 109*
Worth, Stephen, 160
wrists, 115
Wrong Trousers, The (1993), 164
Wustmann, Kurt, *18, 19*

X
x sheets, 179

Y
Yal, Samuel, *149*
Yee, Kristina, *133*

Z
Zeman, Karel, *49*
Zero (2010), 78, *79*

P3 Unilever *Recipe*, Loose Moose Productions. Produced by Glenn Holberton and directed by Andreas de Ridder.

P9, 33, 106, 139, 152, 165 *Sleight of Hand* courtesy of Michael Cusack. Photos on pages 9 and 106 by Jonathan Rossiter ACS. Photos on pages 33, 139, 152 and 165 by Joanne Bouzanis-Selick.

P11, 81, 134, 207 *Toby's Travelling Circus*, A Mackinnon & Saunders production for Komixx Entertainment and Channel 5, directed by Barry Purves.

P12, 99, 145 *Oh Willy…*, © Emma De Swaef and Marc James Roels.

P15 *L'homme a la tête en caoutchouc*, Star Film / The Kobal Collection.

P16 *The Story of the Fox*, Władysław Starewicz Production / The Kobal Collection.

P19 *Pas de Deux,* National Film Board of Canada / The Kobal Collection. *The Chimp Project*, Handspring Puppet Company. Photograph © Ruphin Coudyzer FPPSA.

P23 *Achilles*, a Bare Boards production for Channel Four Television. Still by Paul Stewart. Directed by Barry Purves and produced by Glenn Holberton.

P25, 138 *The Man Who Was Afraid of Falling* © Joseph Wallace and University of Wales, Newport.

P25, 60, 117 *Next*, An Aardman Animations film, stills by Dave Alex Riddet, directed by Barry Purves, produced by Sara Mullock.

P27 *Bobby Yeah* courtesy of Robert Morgan.

P28 *Lost and Found* courtesy of Joan C. Gratz.

P29 *Wife of Bath* (*Canterbury Tales Part 1*) courtesy of Joanna Quinn.

P30 *The Curse of the Were-Rabbit*, Dreamworks / Aardman Animations / The Kobal Collection.

P33 *Billy Twinkle: Requiem for a Golden Boy* courtesy of Ronnie Burkett Theatre of Marionettes. Photography by Trudie Lee.

P35 *I Am Tom Moody* courtesy of Ainslie Henderson (Edinburgh College of Art). Photos by Oliver Henderson.

P37 *King Kong* courtesy of RKO / The Kobal Collection. *King Kong* courtesy of Universal / Wing Nut Films / The Kobal Collection.

P39 *The Thing* (production shot) courtesy of Randall William Cook.

P40 *The Terminator*, Orion / The Kobal Collection.

P42 *Ray Harryhausen: Special Effects Titan* courtesy of The Ray and Diana Harryhausen Foundation.

P43 *The 7th Voyage of Sinbad*, Columbia / The Kobal Collection.

P45, 95, 107 *The Pirates! In an Adventure with Scientists*, Sony Pictures Animation / The Kobal Collection.

P46 *I Live in the Woods* courtesy of Max Winston.

P48 *A Christmas Dream* courtesy of Kratky Film / The Kobal Collection.

P53 *Hamlet,* ITV Global / The Kobal Collection / Wilfred Newton.

P55 *Mask II* by Ron Mueck, image © 2008 Getty Images. Photographer: Peter Macdiarmid.

P56 *Komaneko: The Curious Cat* © TYO / dwarf-Komaneko Film Partners.

P59 *Harvie Krumpet* courtesy of Melodrama Pictures Pty Ltd.

P63 The Nightmare Before Christmas, Touchstone/Burton/Di Novi / The Kobal Collection.

P65 *Alice* (*Něco z Alenky*), Condor Films / The Kobal Collection.

P67 *ParaNorman*, Laika Entertainment / The Kobal Collection.

P68, 71, 111 *Life's a Zoo* created by Adam Shaheen and Andrew Horne II, Cuppa Coffee Studios.

P69 *Animal Farm* courtesy of Vivien Halas. © The Halas & Batchelor Collection Limited.

P70 *Street of Crocodiles* © Koninck Studios Ltd.

P73 *Mary Poppins*, Walt Disney Pictures / The Kobal Collection.

P74 *Balance* courtesy of Christoph and Wolfgang Lauenstein. Nina Conti and Monkey © 2004 Getty Images. Photo by Dave Hogan.

P77 *Slumberless* © 2013 Simon Partington. All rights reserved.

P79 *Zero* images courtesy of Zealous Creative.

P83, 155 *The Maker*, images courtesy of Zealous Creative.

P84 *There There* courtesy of Chris Hopewell © Collision Films.

P85, 209, 215 *Plume* © Dark Prince 2013. Photos by Justin Noe and Stéphane Piera.

P86 *Pipkin* © 2013 Pipkin Productions.

P91, 93, 111, 141, 146, 168, 175 *Tchaikovsky – An Elegy*, a Studio MIR production, 2011. Photos by Joe Clarke and Justin Noe.

P95 *All My Relations* courtesy of Priestley Motion Pictures.

P96 Stop-motion armature kit © Animation Toolkit Ltd 2013.

P97 *Screen Play*, a Bare Boards production for Channel Four Television. Directed, written and animated by Barry Purves. Produced by Glenn Holberton.

P98 *Uncle Creepy* © Chiodo Bros. Productions, Inc.

P100 *The Family Story* courtesy of Chris Walsh.

P101 *The Piper* poster © Daniel James 2013.

P102 *Hinterland* courtesy of Linda McCarthy and Steven Appleby / Tiny Elephants Ltd.

P103–104, 132, 158 *Friendly Fire* courtesy of Andy Kaiser / Rubber Rocket.

P108–109 *Minhocas / Worms* courtesy of Animaking Studios.

P112 *Playing Ghost* courtesy of Bianca Ansems.

P113, 149 *Madame Tutli-Putli* photographs used with permission of the National Film Board of Canada.

P114, 193 *Out on the Tiles* courtesy of Anna Pearson. *In the Fall of Gravity* courtesy of Ron Cole, Wobbly Tripod.

P117 *Tales from the Powder Room* courtesy of Darren Burgess and Anifex Pty Ltd.

P119 *Faust* courtesy of Heart of Europe / Lumen / Athenor / The Kobal Collection. *Beaver Creek* courtesy of Ian Timothy © 2009.

P121 *Mona Lisa Descending a Staircase* courtesy of Joan C. Gratz.

P122, 177 *Una Furtiva Lagrima* courtesy of Carlo Vogele. *Day Shift* © Ian Timothy 2012.

P123 *The Owl who Married a Goose: An Eskimo Legend* Caroline Leaf.

P124 *Bear with Me* courtesy of Uriah Naeh, Bezalel Academy of Arts and Design, Jerusalem.

P125 *Being Bradford Dillman* courtesy of Loose Moose Productions.

P126 *Roots of the Hidden* © Elizabeth Marie Sevenoaks, created at the Arts University Bournemouth.

P128 *Les Trois Inventeurs* courtesy of Michel Ocelot, Studio O. *The Tale of Sir Richard* © Peter Dodd, 2006.

P131, 197 *Mary and Max* courtesy of Melodrama Pictures Pty Ltd.

P133 *Miss Todd* courtesy of Kristina Yee.

P136-137 *Head Over Heels* courtesy of Tim Reckart.

P138 *Goutte d'Or* ©2013, Christophe Peladan, Happy Flyfish 2 and ExFool's Production.

P141 *Electreecity* courtesy of Sarah Barnes and Sarah Duffield-Harding.

P143 *Compost Corner* set, copyright ITV Digital Channels 2013.

P145, 169 *The Gravedigger's Tale* courtesy of Min Young Oh and The National Film and Television School.

P146, 186 *Tomorrow* courtesy of Bob Lee / Siobhan Fenton. Funded by 4mations Digital Shorts scheme © 2009.

P149 *L'Oiseau* © Double Mètre Animation / Samuel Yal.

P150 *Stanley Pickle* © Vicky Mather.

P157 *Viv and Mandy in the Big Clean Up* © Daniel James 2009.

P158–159 *Beneath the Moonlight* courtesy of Enrique Ortega Cortez, Queltehue Producciones.

P161 *I Wish I Went to Ecuador* courtesy of David Bunting and the pupils of Bricknell Primary School.

P163 *Foxed!* poster © Geneva Film Co. 2013.

P166 *Iluzia* courtesy of Uriah Naeh and Udi Asoulin.

P167 *Mother's Song* courtesy of Linda McCarthy. *The Owl House* courtesy of Jessica Cope, The Edinburgh College of Art.

P171 *Lo Guarracino* courtesy of Michelangelo Fornaro.

P173 *Jason and the Argonauts*, Columbia / The Kobal Collection.

P178 *Coraline*, Focus Features / The Kobal Collection.

P179 *Gilbert & Sullivan The Very Models* – a Bare Boards production for Channel Four Television. Photographer: Jean-Marc Ferriere.

P181 *A Life Well Seasoned* courtesy of Daniel Rieley, Arts University Bournemouth.

P182 *Corpse Bride*, Warner Bros / The Kobal Collection.

P184 Paint on glass image courtesy of Caroline Leaf.

P188 *A Midsummer Night's Dream*, Studio Kresceneho / A Loutkoveho Filmu / The Kobal Collection.

P193 Chiodo Brothers set © Chiodo Bros. Productions, Inc.

P195 *Sunday Drive* courtesy of José Miguel Ribeiro © Zeppelin Filmes / S.O.I.L / il Luster / Folimage. Photos by Claudia Guerreiro, Niza and Ana Sequeira.

P201 Dance studies courtesy of David P. France Dance Company.

P203 *War Horse* courtesy of Getty Images © 2012 Ilya S. Savenok.

P205 *Monsterous Murders* courtesy of Sarah Barnes and Sarah Duffield-Harding. *A**hole Robot* courtesy of Chris Walsh and Mad Lab Productions.

For my dear sister, Amanda, and her husband, Peter, who have always helped in so many ways.

Thanks, too, to all the animators, marionettists, puppeteers, performers, producers, dancers, photographers, craftsmen and artists who have generously given me permission to use their beautiful and informative stills.

Finally, thanks to Georges Méliès, who started it all; to Ray Harryhausen, who shared his passion and genius so generously and warmly with us all; and finally to Mark Hall, who let it happen for me.